Prayer and Life's Highest

Prayer and Life's Highest

PAUL STROMBERG REES

Pastor of First Covenant Church, Minneapolis, Minnesota

WM. B. EERDMANS PUBLISHING COMPANY
GRAND RAPIDS   1956   MICHIGAN

First published 1956

Printed in the United States of America

To
Evelyn
Methodist Minister's
Wife
Mother of
"Melissa" and "Meg Ann"
The First Dear
Creature in
This Mysterious Universe
To Call Me "Father"

CONTENTS

PRAYER AND THE WAY OF MASTERY

"Wherefore I also, after I heard of your faith in the Lord Jesus, and love unto all the saints, Cease not to give thanks for you, making mention of you in my prayers; That the God of our Lord Jesus Christ, the Father of glory, may give unto you the spirit of wisdom and revelation in the knowledge of him: The eyes of your understanding being enlightened: that ye may know what is the hope of his calling, and what the riches of the glory of his inheritance in the saints, And what is the exceeding greatness of his power to us-ward who believe, according to the working of his mighty power."

Ephesians 1 : 15–19.

"For this cause I bow my knees unto the Father of our Lord Jesus Christ, Of whom the whole family in heaven and earth is named, That he would grant you, according to the riches of his glory, to be strengthened with might by his Spirit in the inner man; That Christ may dwell in your hearts by faith; that ye, being rooted and grounded in love, May be able to comprehend with all saints what is the breadth, and length, and depth, and height; And to know the love of Christ, which passeth knowledge, that ye might be filled with all the fulness of God."

Ephesians 3 : 14–19.

I

PRAYER AND THE WAY OF MASTERY

PROF. JAMES STEWART has a study of St. Paul, entitled *A Man In Christ*. In the opening chapter he makes the observation that modern views of St. Paul tend to swing between two extremes: one, in which the apostle is held to have been first, last, and all the time a theologian; and another, in which he is seen as no theologian at all.

The truth, says Stewart, makes its home with neither extreme. On the one hand Paul was not in the technical sense a systematic theologian nor, on the other, was he a dreamer, a mystic, "satisfied with emotion, sentiment or ecstasy."

In his discussion of this matter Professor Stewart uses a phrase that flashes light on a facet of Paul's ministry with which we shall be occupied in these studies. The phrase is this: "the exigencies of his pastoral duties." There you have, in a capsule, the historical, personal, and passionate background of the prayers that rose from the pastorally concerned soul of Christ's greatest apostle.

At least a dozen of these prayers—make it thirteen if you insist on a Pauline authorship for Hebrews—have been woven by the Spirit of God into the fabric of Paul's writings. We shall content ourselves with a study of six of these devotional and intercessory classics. Even this restricted field will put us in possession of wealth so vast as to leave us quite breathless.

For, mind you, if this man Paul was mighty and massive as a man of *thought*, and as a man of *action*, and as a man of *vision*, and as a man of *eloquence*, he was mighty and massive also as a man of *prayer*. Indeed, from the point of view of his *Christian* creativeness and effectiveness it **was be-cause** he *was* a man of prayer that *thought* and *action* and *vision* and *eloquence* took on the towering significance that they had in his God-appointed career. For him prayer was no ritual dulness; it was robust dynamic. It was not verbal patter but veritable power.

Exactly sixty years ago a London publisher issued a book by a theologian, W. B. Pope, under the title *The Prayers of St. Paul*. Pope feels that the prayers which are recorded in the Pauline letters stamp these documents as unique. "If we except the Book of Psalms," says he, "which is expressly the universal Liturgy of the Bible, nothing like it is observed in any other writer of Holy Scripture."

We enter, therefore, an extraordinarily hallowed enclosure as now we turn to the first two of the prayers that will have our attention in this series. These come in the Ephesian letter and, though they are separated by a chapter, are so related that they may be subsumed under the one head of "Prayer and Life's Mastery."

To be perfectly fair and frank with any who are especially interested in New Testament research and historical origins, may I say that, in my view, the long accepted Pauline author-ship of Ephesians is not overthrown by the alleged evidence put forward by certain contemporary scholars. I have read the case for repudiation as it is presented, for example, in *The Interpreter's Bible*. Without making any claim to scholarship, I nevertheless must say that the "proof" of a non-Pauline authorship seems unconvincing.

Paul is our man! Paul has had a long term of ministry in Ephesus. The place and the people are dear to him. But he is now a prisoner in Rome. Yonder are his Christian friends not only in the city of Ephesus but, in all probability, in sur-rounding communities. He wants to communicate with them.

Fortunately, there are no heresies by which their minds are being poisoned, nor are there any quarrels by which their fellowship is being sundered or shattered. The shepherd-heart of the apostle can therefore go out to them along the lines that are sunny, serene, and sublime. He can write to inspire and confirm them, to envision and elevate them.

And as he writes (or dictates), he *prays*. One thing, beyond all others, is central in his praying for them: they must realize how amazingly *adequate* they are to be, how *masterfully* they can live, if only they will appropriate the boundless resources that are theirs in Christ.

Take this as the diamond-centre of the first prayer: "that ye may know what is the hope of his calling, and what the riches of the glory of his inheritance in the saints, and what is the exceeding greatness of his power to us-ward who believe" (1: 18, 19).

Take this as the potent heart of the second prayer: "that he would grant you, according to the riches of his glory, to be strengthened with might by his Spirit in the inner man" (3: 16).

Prayer for masterful living—that's what we have here. Prayer for Christians that they may find in Christ, since they cannot find it anywhere else, the ability to cope with life, to beat down "principalities and powers," to turn back the onrush of temptation, to outwit the machinations of the devil, to subdue and regulate the instinctual drives of human nature, to fasten to the Cross the false ego that so stubbornly resists its doom—what prayer for mastery this is!

While the two prayers are similar, and both focus upon this matter of abounding adequacy in Christian living, our treatment of them will be one in which, in the first instance, the stress will fall on the *revelation* of that mastery which Christ provides for us, while in the second petition the accent drops on the *realization* of this mastery in actual experience.

To state the case differently, Paul first prays that these pilgrims of the Lord might walk the way of *light,* for without light they cannot know how vast and wonderful is the inheritance that has already fallen to them in virtue of their union with Christ. In the second petition he asks that they may walk the way of *love,* since no man, nor any community of men bearing the name Christian, can exhibit victoriousness that is Christlike without being "rooted and grounded in love."

I. Consider, then, the first prayer, and its key-thought of *revelation*.

Examine, to start with, the *mood* in which the apostle makes his intercession. This may be discovered by giving attention to two parts of the prayer, one in which he addresses the Ephesians, and the other in which he addresses God. Of them he says, in verses 15, 16, "Wherefore I also, after I heard of your faith in the Lord Jesus, and love unto all the saints, cease not to give thanks for you." Of God he says, in verse 17, "the God of our Lord Jesus Christ, the Father of glory."

Thus the apostle's mood is one in which, thinking of those *for* whom he prays, he is *thankful*; and, thinking of the God *to* whom he prays, he is *thrilled*.

When Paul thought of the Galatians, he felt like sighing; when he thought of these Ephesians, he felt like singing. You and I have had some experience with these differences between Christians. We too have known those whose waywardness has made us weep, whose backslidings have broken our hearts. But then we too have witnessed the opposite. We have seen those whose early faith was made firm, whose humility of spirit held promise of bright tomorrows, whose eagerness to climb the high trails with Christ was keen, and we have found prayer for them a kind of doxology.

Prayer in the mood of thanksgiving is a flavourful, even as it is a forceful, thing.

But the Paul of the *thankful* heart as he contemplated these Christian comrades was also the Paul of the *thrilled* heart as he faced God. Do you not instantly catch something of his exultant spirit as he represents himself addressing the Deity by the dual title of "the God of our Lord Jesus Christ" and "the Father of glory"?

Don't expect Paul to give you stereotypes! What we might have looked for here is "the Father of our Lord Jesus" and "the God of glory." But the apostle, always good for a surprise, switches the terms in such a way that each title stands alone in the New Testament: "the God of our Lord Jesus" and "the Father of glory." He is the God to whom Jesus as the perfect Man gave worship, calling Him, "my God" (John 20: 17). But He is more. He is the God whom Jesus as the sinless Son incarnately revealed.

This God is "the Father of glory." Members of God's family, draw near! Here is *your* God, replete with a fatherliness tender enough to attract a child, and radiant with a glory—an embodiment of all perfections—ineffable enough to prostrate a saint.

In such a mood of wonder and worship the little man yonder in Rome lifts up his heart in intercession.

Turn now to consider the *medium* through which this prayer is to be answered. My concern, says the apostle, is that "the God of our Lord Jesus Christ, the Father of glory, may give unto you the Spirit of wisdom and revelation in the knowledge of him" (v. 17). I capitalize the word "Spirit" for I believe (with Dean Alford, Pope, Blaikie, Beare and others) that the reference is to the Holy Spirit.

Alford and Blaikie are probably right when they suggest that what Paul really comprehends here is neither the Holy Spirit apart from the spirit of man nor the spirit of man apart from the Holy Spirit, but rather the Christian concept of man's renewed spirit as indwelt, and moved, by God's Spirit. Recall our Lord's word concerning the Holy Spirit: "He shall take of mine and shall show it unto you" (John 16: 15). He is the Agent of enlightenment.

The words "wisdom" and "revelation" are closely coupled, yet distinct. Pope's comment is apt, it seems to me: "the Spirit is the giver of revelation objectively and the source of wisdom subjectively." They are two sides of one coin. On one side you see Peter, for example, at the house of Simon in Joppa, confronted by the vision of the sheet filled with clean and unclean creatures. That was the revelation looked at *objectively*—the thing revealed.

But what did it signify? The meaning of it, subjectively, came only as Peter reflected on it. In Acts 10: 19 we read, "While Peter thought on the vision, the Spirit saith unto him, Beloved, three men seek thee." First, the revelation, then the wisdom by which its significance is grasped!

In fine consistency with this position Paul's prayer makes reference next to the *marvels* which he longs to have unveiled to these young believers at Ephesus. Three quite wonderful disclosures will be made to them in just the measure in which their spiritual eyes, their "eyes for invisibles," are opened. "The eyes of your understanding" in the King James Version becomes, almost without exception, "the eyes of your hearts" in later translations. Thus long before Pascal said it St. Paul knew it: "The heart has its reasons, which reason knows not." Not, "mere intellectual acuteness, but a flooding of the whole inward being with the light of divine truth"—this is the apostle's desire for the young church at Ephesus.

The threefold answer to the prayer finds its simple symbol in the triple use of the word "what." "That ye may know"—

   (i) "*What* is the hope of your calling," and
  (ii) "*What* the riches of the glory of his inheritance in the saints," and
 (iii) "*What* is the exceeding greatness of his power to us-ward who believe."

(i) Something to *enhearten* us—"hope." In the nearest thing to a formal definition of faith that the Scriptures afford us, Hebrews 11: 1, there is a blending of "faith" and "hope": "Now faith is the substance of things hoped for, evidence of things not seen." Let me put it this way: faith as to the *fact* of our salvation ("Christ died for our sins," 1 Cor. 15: 3) becomes *experience;* faith as to the *fruition* of our salvation ("unto them that look for him shall he appear the second time without sin unto salvation," Hebrews 9: 28) becomes *expectation.* Here is our hope.

Someone has defined hope as "a compound emotion that consists of desire and expectation." To expect without desire is dread; to desire without expectation is despair. Unite the two, and hope leaps up!

O Christians, cries Paul, God has ordained that "in the dispensation of the fulness of times" He will "gather together in one all things in Christ, both which are in heaven, and which are on earth" (v. 10). Do you desire that? Do you expect it? You may. You should. For it is the hope to which God has called you.

The general hopelessness of the world of Paul's day has been remarked by many a historian. The philosophical cynicism then current had a certain glitter about it, to be sure. Still, it was hopeless. The popular mood, however, was without gleam or grandeur. History held neither purpose nor goal, neither focus nor fulfilment. Its gloom-obsessed prophet might well have been our modern Bertrand Russell with his lugubrious prose elegy: "Brief and powerless is Man's life; on him and all his race the slow, sure doom falls pitiless and dark."

Leave out God and His Christ, Paul would say, and that is the philosophy of meaninglessness to which you are pitiably reduced. But see what happens when you put Christ in there, where indeed God has put Him—incarnate, crucified, resurrected, ascended, and, one day, to be unveiled in His glory. In Him is the clue to history. He is the summing up of all things. This phrasing in fact carries out the meaning of the Greek word that in the King James Version is translated "gather together in one." It may be rendered either "to head up" or "to sum up."

History without Christ, says Paul, is like adding a column of figures endlessly, without ever arriving at a total. God will not have it so. "The mystery of his will," now revealed in a way that the unenlightened Bertrand Russell mind would never grasp in a million years, is that Christ is at once the focus and fulfilment of all history, all experience, all creation. Here is hope that "maketh not ashamed."

B

(ii) Consider another marvel that Paul prays will be unveiled to these Ephesians: "what the riches of the glory of
his inheritance in the saints." If the first "what" presents
something to enhearten us, this one presents something to
enrich us. By stating the point thus you may gain the im-
pression that I have chosen to come down strictly on one side
of the two interpretations that may be given to this clause.
Is this a reference to God's heritage in His people or to their
heritage in Him? Judging by the comments of the scholars,
the Greek can be construed either way.

Twice before in this chapter, in verses 11 and 14, the word
"inheritance" has been introduced. After examining both
passages Professor Findlay observes: the apostle "plays upon
the double aspect of the inheritance, regarded now as the
heritage of the saints in God and again as His heritage in
them."

Suppose you say that God finds His wealth and glory in
His redeemed people. They are, let us agree, His "peculiar
treasure," following the language used to describe His covenant people in the Old Testament. They are "a people for
his own possession," following Peter's phrasing in 1 Peter
2: 9. Is it not true that this very great fact means also the
enrichment, the unimaginable enhancement, of those who
are the subjects of His redemption and the objects of His
affection and pleasure?

Let us imagine that Her Majesty the Queen, acting through
proper channels, decided that a competent young lady in
this audience would be useful and valuable as a member of
the secretarial staff of Buckingham Palace. Imagine—and I'm
sure you have no difficulty in so doing—what this would
mean by way of enhancement to the young lady. To be sure,
she is only one of many subordinate secretaries. Still, she is
rated as having value to the Queen. But that very fact, together with the new relationship it carries with it, does
something to her value: it immensely increases it. She is
one of the *Queen's* secretaries! Similarly, God has given the
Church to His Son as the Son's inheritance. The Church is

Christ's bride! Christ is rich in His bride; the bride is rich in her Lover. The glory of this richness fills Paul with wide-eyed wonder, and he wants this adoring amazement to possess the souls of the Ephesian believers.

(iii) Then—following on in a crescendo effect—the apostle prays that their enlightened eyes will behold "what is the exceeding greatness of his power to us-ward who believe." Something to enhearten us? Yes. Something to enrich us? Yes. And now, in addition, something to *energize* us.

Here is the capstone of the prayer. Without this the eyes of the Christian heart would not see enough. We may cherish high hopes, but what if they turn out to be but a tissue of idle dreams? We may exult in the wealth of the heritage that we have in Christ and He in us, but what if that heritage is made shabby and is wasted by mean carnalities and trampling defeats and a generally uninspiring spectacle of spiritual ineffectualness?

Do we not rightly ask: By what means are we to march steadily toward the fulfilment of the hope set before us? By what resources can the glory of the inheritance be kept from fading?

The full answer comes in one of those tremendous sentences for which St. Paul is famous—embracing in the Authorized Version not less than five verses. The potent core of it, however, lies in the initial clause which, in the Revised Standard Version, reads: "what is the immeasurable greatness of his power in us who believe."

At that point the Apostle's surging soul begins to strain at the leash of language. It is immeasurable, he seems to say. Yet if I must give you some yardsticks by which to gauge its greatness, I will put these three in your hands:

(a) It is *resurrection* power—the power God "wrought in Christ when he raised him from the dead."

(b) It is *ascension* power—"and set him at his own right hand in the heavenly places."

(c) It is *dominion* power—"far above all principality, and power, and might, and dominion . . . and hath put all things under his feet, and gave him to be the head over all things to the church."

Now return to verse 19 a moment. Here in one swift clause are four different power words. First the principal term, *dunamis*, "power"—from which we get our English word "dynamite." Then, in the clause in which Paul strains to spell out for us the unutterable amplitude and adeqaucy of this power, he says, literally, "according to the working (*energeia*) of the power (*kratos*) of his might (*ischus*)." Dunamis, the inclusive term, speaks of ability to achieve. *Energeia* suggests action, power at work. *Kratos* signifies power that subdues, rules, governs. *Ischus*, finally, hints at power that is inherent, that resides in a person whether he uses it or not.

All of that goes into my prayer for you, writes Paul. All of that is in Christ, through the Holy Spirit, for you. The power of mastery through your being joined to Him who is forever the Master.

So closes the first prayer in the Ephesian letter. It is the prayer for *revelation*. The enlightened church is to discover what marvels God has put within her grasp. There is hope that *beckons* her. There is an inheritance that *blesses* her. There is power that *backs* her.

II. The second Ephesian prayer, as I have already suggested, is likewise concerned with masterful Christian living, but here the stress is upon *realization*. Spiritual mastery *exhibited* as our privilege and right is good; spiritual mastery *experienced* as our practice and joy is better.

In the first prayer the apostle makes no reference to posture. In this he does: he is the *kneeling* pastor! "I bow my knees!" Luke, you remember, tells us that when Paul had finished his last and solemnly tender message to the elders of this Ephesian church, on the occasion of his brief stop at the port of Miletus, "he kneeled down, and prayed with them all" (Acts 20: 36). Perhaps the prevailing posture of Bible times *was* standing. Be it so. There are occasions, nevertheless, when nothing seems quite so becoming as the action of kneeling. God's ultimate majesty is deserving of such a sign. Our clamant need accords well with such a symbol. But then, in any case, I would not press too far the *physical* posture. Jerome's fine phrase of long ago must not be forgotten—"the knees of the mind."

I shall not ask you to join in any elaborate discussion of the disputed meaning that attaches to the title "the Father ... of whom the whole family in heaven and earth is named." Most of our versions since the Authorized substitute "every family" for "the whole family." This makes the meaning *distributive* rather than *collective*. It is then interpreted by some as a reference to the "family" of angels, which "in heaven" calls God "Father," and to the "family" of believers, which on "earth" calls God "Father."

The weight of scholarly opinion and evidence seems to fall on the side of the distributive rather than collective meaning. Actually, in the Greek there is a play on words—*patria* for "family" and *Pater* for "Father"—that is difficult to carry over into English. What is suggested is that wherever you find a true family relationship there you find a fatherhood of which God, in His relation either to angels or redeemed men, is the supreme example. This thought Phillips has endeavoured to capture by following the title "God the Father" with a parenthesis which reads, "from whom all fatherhood, earthly or heavenly, derives its name."

We come now to the specific petitions of this lofty prayer. Whether we make their number *three*, as some do, or *four*, or *six*, will depend on our understanding of the force of the participial clauses. Some have sought the key to the enumeration of the petitions in the word "that." In the Authorized Version it appears four times:

1. "*That* he would grant you ... to be strengthened with might by his Spirit in the inner man."
2. "*That* Christ may dwell in your hearts by faith."

3. *"That* ye may be able to comprehend . . . and to know the love of Christ."
4. *"That* ye might be filled with all the fulness of God."

This scheme of analysis has neatness, but it overlooks a problem. In the Greek text the clause rendered "that Christ may dwell in your hearts by faith" has no word for "that." Hence the scholars, if you consult them, will take you on a merry-go-round of opinions as to whether verse 17 should be connected with verse 16 as a consequence or with verse 18 as a cause. Some would make Paul say: *"Since* the Holy Spirit is yours for empowerment, you will realize what it truly means for Christ to dwell in you." Others would make him say: *"Because* Christ dwells in you, 'you may have power,' as the RSV puts it, 'to comprehend with all saints . . . and to know the love of Christ which surpasses knowledge.'"

The scheme that I venture to suggest takes as a key the three-fold use (in the Greek text) of the "that."

1. *Paul asks for the power of God's Spirit:* "that he would grant you . . . to be strengthened with might by his Spirit."

Someone has said that there are just two great human needs: 'light on the mystery of life and life for the mastery of life.' Here, in the Holy Spirit, is life, energy, limitless vitality, for the mastery of life.

Western culture to-day has done much to eliminate mystery —the mystery of the combustion engine, the mystery of germs in disease, the mystery of electricity, the mystery of the atom. But western culture has done little to gain mastery. International relations are a tense stalemate. Private morals are in a shabby condition. Nerves are twitchy and jumpy. Fears are innumerable and destructive.

The Church, too, is much less than the community of power it ought to be. Even evangelicalism can be at once doctrinally immaculate and disastrously impotent. Our theological hair-splittings stand us in poor stead when we obviously lack the grace of sweet temper, the capacity for taking criticism without going into an emotional funk, or the generosity that puts the better of two possible constructions on something said or done by a fellow Christian.

The power of Acts 1 : 8 is patently missing: "Ye shall receive power after that the Holy Ghost is come upon you." I know you have been made *alive* by the Spirit, Paul would say; but have you been made *adequate* by the Spirit? The very same Holy Spirit who infuses life imparts power.

Mark the *extent* of this power which God communicates through His Spirit. It is "according to the riches of his glory" (v. 16). It is not said that the power He gives is "out of" but "according to" what Moffatt calls "the wealth of his glory." If you had nothing, and dire need were pinching you, while a friend of yours had a hundred thousand pounds; and if that friend sent you a ten shilling note, what he gave you would be "out of" his riches, but it would *not* be "according to" his riches. It is never so with God. As Adam Clarke put it, "God acts up to the dignity of His perfections."

Mark too the *effect* of this empowerment by the Spirit. It is that "Christ may dwell in your hearts by faith" (v. 17). That He may "make his home" there, is the Arthur Way rendering. You can find plenty of people whose heart is like a *tavern*, where Christ finds no welcome, where evil plies its trade busily and brazenly. You can find others whose heart is like a *hotel* with rooms all parcelled out, and a rather nice one assigned to the Lord Jesus. You can find yet others whose heart is like a *home*, where Christ the Lord has been given not only the right of entry but the right of mastery. There's not a room He cannot occupy, not a corner He cannot inspect, not a piece of furniture He cannot either enjoy or remove!

Observe, further, the *excellence* of his power, which is so limitless in its extent and so Christ-glorifying in its effect: "being rooted and grounded in love" (v. 17). "The inward power imparted by the Spirit," says Beare, "and the abiding presence of Christ in the heart result in a life rooted and grounded in love." This is linked closely with what follows.

2. *Paul asks for the practice of God's love.* The second "that" comes in the Greek at the beginning of verse 18: "that ye may be able to comprehend," or, better still, to "grasp" or "seize," "what is the breadth, and length, and depth, and height" of God's whole redemptive plan and provision, and especially "to know the love of Christ, which passeth knowledge."

Both "comprehend" and "know" in this passage reach far beyond the intellectual or the theoretical. They carry us right over into the realm of experience and practice. Here indeed is the wedding of "knowledge" and "love" in a life that is love-controlled.

Such a love and such a life spell mastery or they spell nothing. They represent the enabling of the indwelling Christ through His Spirit. I have long been charmed and, I may add, chastened by the life-story of Henry Martyn, but it came alive for me with extraordinary vividness as I read recently a moving résumé of it.

With his brilliant student career at Cambridge behind him, there came the call of his Lord to the mission field. Though several attractive, lucrative vocations were open to him, he said: "Here I am, Lord: send me to the ends of the earth; send me to the rough, the savage pagans of the wilderness; send me from all that is called comfort in earth; send me even to death itself if it but be in Thy service and in Thy kingdom."

When he fell deeply in love with a girl named Lydia, he told her of his call from God to live and minister in India. Was this agreeable to her? He pleaded that it might be. It was not. If he would stay in England, he could have her as his bride. If he went to India, it would be without her. Hence the question, like a drum-beat in his brain: "India or Lydia? Lydia or India? . . ."

But Martyn was a mastered man—mastered by love and love's Master. Therefore the mastery was his in a crisis of poignant choice. Pain-drenched yet triumphant was his witness: "My dear Lydia and my duty call me different ways.

Yet God hath not forsaken me. . . . I am born for God only. Christ is nearer to me than father or mother or sister."

And here, of course, enters the paradox: such love, "surpasses knowledge" (RSV). However tremendously or transformingly we may experience it, it has depths that defy us, heights that haunt us. How could it be otherwise, since it is so divine a gift? It is nothing less than Christ's love in us awakening a responsive love which we give back to Him.

> *It passeth knowledge, that dear love of Thine,*
> *My Jesus, Saviour; yet this soul of mine*
> *Would of Thy love, in all its breadth and length,*
> *Its height and depths, and everlasting strength,*
> *Know more and more.*

3. Finally—in ravishing climax—*Paul asks for the plenitude of God Himself*: "That ye might be filled with all the fulness of God" (v. 19).

Language is about to break down. The wings of Paul's prayer become pinions that dare the ultimate. The zenith is not beyond his soaring.

But what is meant? No *absurdity*, for one thing. Paul was mystical, but always within limits. The creature, even the redeemed creature, remains always a creature; the Creator remains forever the Creator. The lines are not exclusive and yet they are never rubbed out.

What is meant? No *impossibility*, for another thing. Or, to make my meaning clearer, no *present* impossibility. Spiritual goods intended by our Lord for present consumption are by many of us shipped ahead to some storage depot in the shadowland of death or the gloryland of heaven!

What is meant? Supernatural *reality*, let us call it. God Himself as communicable to men, possessing their no longer rebel or alien hearts! Anything else? Yes. With God Himself, His gifts of grace and guidance, as communicable to, and fashioned for, the community of the redeemed—the Church! For "of his fulness have all received, and grace for grace" (John 1 : 16).

Can we *contain* God's fulness? No. Can we *receive* it—up to the full measure of our always limited, yet ever enlarging, capacity? Yes.

Looking at it *gift*-wise, it may be a reception as sudden as the filling with the Spirit that came to the disciples on Pentecost. Looking at it *growth*-wise, it must be as progressive and expansive as Paul's word in the following chapter requires, when he says that "speaking the truth in love," we "may grow up into him in all things, which is the head, even Christ" (4: 15).

So, in the atmosphere and exercise of prayer, we come to the close of our first walk along this "way of mastery." "Brothers," cries Paul, "do know of my intense concern for you. You tend to 'faint' (v. 13), either because of your own sufferings or mine. Faint not! The Christian is not called to be victim but victor. The Church of our Lord is not called to feebleness or futility but to mastery. Let God reveal to you the immeasurable resources that He has made yours in His Son. But more, let Him lead you from revelation to realization. And if you are tempted to doubt what I now write to you, look at God! Look at God!

Why?

Because He is "able"!

"He is able to do!"

"He is able to do exceeding abundantly!"

"He is able to do exceeding abundantly above all that we ask or think, according to the power that worketh in us!"

I shall never forget the comment once made by an eloquent Welsh preacher whom I loved, who, taking this little word "able," drew it out in a glorious acrostic:

"*A*lmighty
*B*oundless
*L*imitless
*E*verlasting . . . Power!"

To that one can only add the Pauline "Amen!"

PRAYER AND THE WAY OF EXCELLENCY

"And this I pray, that your love may abound yet more and more in knowledge and in all judgment; That ye may approve things that are excellent; that ye may be sincere and without offence till the day of Christ; Being filled with the fruits of righteousness, which are by Jesus Christ, unto the glory and praise of God."

Philippians 1 : 9–11

II

PRAYER AND THE WAY OF EXCELLENCY

IN the paragraph of comment which he offers as a preface
to his translation of Philippians, Weymouth calls attention
to the fact that this is "the most intimate of all Paul's
letters to his churches." Evidences of this are not far to seek;
they appear early in the epistle. One is struck with the cordial
warmth and gracious affection of such statements and senti-
ments as these: "I thank my God upon every remembrance
of you, always in every prayer of mine for you all making
request with joy, for your fellowship in the gospel from the
first day until now."

I suppose we might call this a case of "love at first sight!"
Certainly those words, "your fellowship in the gospel from
the first day until now," have a way of seizing one's imagination and sending it marching. That "first day" made history
—the day when Paul and Silas entered Philippi as their initial
field of battle after the invasion of Europe.

What Philippi had lacked in the size of its population it
had made up in the drama of its history and the pride of its
tradition. Named after Philip of Macedon, it was in Paul's
day a Roman colony. Here, on this Macedonian terrain, one
of the most brilliant and formidable military devices of
the ancient world had been worked out—the "Macedonian
Phalanx." It was a formation of men and spears which, in
motion, was so rhythmic, invincible, and terrifying that one
writer said of it, "As it manœuvred over uneven terrain it
looked like a great porcupine with its quills bristling."

Here, too, Alexander the Great had won his first spurs and
from the vicinity of Philippi had moved out and on to world
conquest.

Here Alexander's crack regiment, famous as the "Silver Shields," had come into being. So appalling a name did they gain for themselves that scarce any foe dared stand up to them.

Here too, in Paul's day, were the veterans from the Roman army of Mark Anthony. Not more than a decade before the Apostle's arrival in Philippi Anthony and Octavian, the latter destined to become Emperor Augustus Caesar, had clashed in furious battle with Brutus and Cassius following the assassination of Julius Caesar. This in fact was called the "Battle of Philippi," which ended in the defeat of Brutus and Cassius and signalled the end of the Roman republic.

This was Philippi! This was the city that he and Silas entered on that "first day" to which he makes tender reference as now, years later, he writes to his Philippian friends from the scene of his imprisonment in Rome. On that "first day" the Apostle had found no synagogue, had therefore inquired if there were any Jews in the city, and had received the information that there were some women who were in the habit of meeting on the river bank at the edge of the city on the sabbath. On that "first day"—which we need not confine to a day of twenty-four hours—the Apostle had told the story of Jesus to these curious, wistful, and eventually persuaded women, among whom was Lydia, "whose heart the Lord opened."

On that "first day" there had been persecution of the evangelists, and a brutal beating, and a merciless imprisonment and then, topping it all, a victory as with trumpets and banners! The jailor, newly converted to Christ, became one of the witnessing members of the growing Christian community in Philippi.

Do you wonder that Paul loved these friends of his with a tender and passionate fondness? Or are you surprised that they were so intensely devoted to him that, concerned about his material needs, they should have collected an offering and sent it to him by Epaphroditus? Now, acknowledging their gift, he assures them, "I have you in my heart" (v. 7).

Then, in a direct approach to the prayer we are about to examine, the Apostle says, "God knows how much I long, with deepest Christian love and affection, for your companionship" (v. 8, Phillips).

This tender and profound concern shapes itself into prayer. The prayer in turn ranges over that vast and varied territory into which all Christian lovers have been brought and of which they are to make themselves increasingly the possessors: "this I pray, that your love may abound yet more and more in knowledge and in all judgment; that ye may approve things that are excellent."

Love as the key to life's excellency! That is the theme of the Pauline intercession. What an immense prayer it is! And what an invigorating vision it opens to every child of the Father's love-linked family! While the Apostle is praying we catch something of the immensity, the challenging expansiveness, of the life that is invaded, illumined, and impelled by the redeeming love of God in Christ our Lord.

There are three simple heads under which I want to consider this outpouring of the apostolic heart. Let us think of it, first, as a prayer for *love,* second, as a prayer for *light,* and, third, as a prayer for *life.*

I

First of all, and most obviously, it is a prayer for *love:* "And this I pray, that your love may abound yet more and more."

Three questions bid for attention:

1. *What does St. Paul mean by "love"?* In our English language love is an appallingly overworked word. It speaks both the beauty and the poverty of our mother tongue. The Greeks had four words for love, whereas the sons of Shakespeare and the daughters of Webster have one. So, whether it be the infatuation of an adolescent boy and girl under a summer moon, or the fifth marriage of a four-times divorced Hollywood actress, or what a mother reveals when she risks

her life to rescue her infant child from a building in flames, or an "affair" of illicit passion, or a missionary abandoning the comforts of home for the crudities of life in the African bush, or the Son of God on a Roman gibbet hanging stark against a darkened sky—no matter, we call it "love"!

Our lingual poverty is both a liability and a pity. Hence our need of definition.

The word for love which the New Testament reserves for high and holy purposes is *agape*. God's love for man—*agape*! The Christian's love for God—*agape*! And, much of the time, the Christian's love for others—*agape*!

It is a word that the New Testament lifts out of obscurity into immortality. There was a word for immoral passion. There was a word for sexual feeling. There was a word for fraternal and family affection. All these are passed over in favour of a term that has in it a minimum of *emotion* and a maximum of *evaluation*. Close to its original meaning is the thought of *respect* and associated with this respect is the idea of *preference*.

Such New Testament writers as St. Paul and St. John read the meaning of this word in the mighty *acts* of God, Who chose to do something in Christ never done before and never to be done again: to be *born*, to *live*, to *teach*, to *suffer*, to *die*, to *rise again*—all "for us men and for our salvation."

This God has done because of His express concern for His human creatures, whose rebellion and pride left Him no motive for doing so save only the spontaneous and unmerited favour that He was impelled to show them.

Love, then, in the Pauline sense, is the *redeeming God* saying to His world of lost men, "I prize you so much that I choose, on my own initiative, to bear the cost of your salvation." That is primary. Love, further, is the *redeemed man* saying, "O God, Who in Christ I see upon that Cross, I choose Thee, I prize Thee, above all things else, and shall make Thee my desire and joy world without end." That is secondary; that follows as a sequence.

Love, once more, is the *redeemed community*—the Church

—saying, each to the other and all to their fellows, "I see you as one who, equally with myself, has the price of blood upon you, even the blood of our Lord Jesus Christ, and I therefore prize you, for His sake and your own, and choose to show you that compassionate goodwill that He first showed to me in dying for me."

Clearly, all this is far removed from love as mere emotion, love as blind infatuation, love as sentimental confraternity, love as patriotic attachment. Years ago, in one of William Clow's fine books, I read a sentence on love to which I have returned in my thinking times without number: "Love is that insight and sympathy which craves to bless and delights to commune." To me it is a singularly luminous sentence. I think of Paul, saying, "The Son of God loved me, and gave himself for me." Why? Because he passionately craved to *bless* me and, blessing me with His forgiveness, to *commune* with me, to walk with me, to make me the confidant of His heart and the agent of His purposes.

But that, you say, is defining His love to me. He *can* bless me. What meaning has this definition as applied to my love to Him? Gently, shall I say, as Jesus once did, "You do err, not knowing the Scripture"? Have you forgotten your Psalter: "*Bless* the Lord, O my soul, and all that is within me, bless his holy name" (Psalm 103: 1)? Have you forgotten the Apostle James, who assures us that the dedicated tongue is a member concerning which we may say, "Therewith *bless* we God" (James 3: 9)?

To be sure, we cannot "bless" Him in the same way or degree in which He can bless us, but obviously, by our worship and obedience, we do, in some mysterious fashion, contribute to His joy and enrichment.

Love! What a word it is that Jesus Christ has put upon our lips. And when all of our faltering efforts to define it have exhausted themselves, we can but fall back on the hymn couplet:

> *The love of Jesus, what it is,*
> *None but His loved ones know.*

c

2. Our second question is: *What does St. Paul want us to understand by this phrase, "you love"?* "This I pray, that your love may abound yet more and more."

If you are not accustomed to the disconcerting way in which the expositors can disagree among themselves, I hesitate to send you off with the counsel that you consult them. Some will tell you that the apostle is referring to the love that these Philippian Christians had for him. Others will want you to believe that he means their love for each other. Others will suggest that he speaks of their love to the Lord. Others still will advise you that he means their love for the Lord's service, as exemplified by the collection they had gathered and had forwarded to him.

It may not be any cutting of the Gordian knot—some may even call it a side-stepping of the issue—but I am greedy enough to want something of *all* these meanings as I reflect on this simple but pregnant phrase. "Your love!" Your grasp of God's love to you in Christ! Your responsive love to Him! Your correlative love towards one another and towards me! Your joyous abandon to the Lord's service! The healthy growth of *all* these rich components of the Divine *agape*—this is my prayer for you! Or so, at any rate, I would interpret the apostle's words.

3. And now our third question: *What does our praying Apostle mean by the words, "abound yet more and more"?* So learned and able a commentator as Meyer contends, on technical, grammatical grounds, that these words modify, not "your love," but the terms "knowledge" and "discernment" that follow.

Not having either the learning or the time to discuss the technical aspects of the matter, I am content here to say that my view of the question is determined by those scholars who find Meyer's argument unconvincing. Growth in love is not excluded from Paul's thought. Indeed, to exclude it would appear to run counter to the emphatic way in which Paul elsewhere asks us to think of love as being central to all spiritual development. For example, he tells the Ephesian

Christians: "We are to hold by the truth, and by our love to grow up wholly into him" (4: 15, Moffatt). And he tells the Corinthian believers, "While knowledge may make a man look big, it is only love that can make him grow to his full stature" (I Cor. 8: 1, Phillips).

The word for "abound" in our passage suggests a river overflowing its banks. It deepens and widens. Its overflow is without confines.

Your life in Christ is to be like that, says St. Paul. Never be satisfied to have His love *abiding* in you. Let it be *abounding*.

Overflow your present *capacity* to love. Not one of us has reached the limit of it. It is all but infinite.

Overflow your present *understanding* of love. New insights into its meaning and mystery will never cease coming to you if you are open to them.

Overflow your present *range* of love. Live in an expanding circle of contacts and challenges. Take in more persons and more situations, to whose needs you make response.

For, after all:

> *Living is loving,*
> *Loving is giving,*
> *Giving is growing,*
> *Growing is God.*

In the life of love there are no "Pillars of Hercules." You remember how the proud men of Spain in the days of the empire struck off their coins with the Pillars of Hercules engraved and the words *"Ne Plus Ultra"* inscribed. "Nothing beyond!" What a colossal irony when, in fact, the whole vast, heaving Atlantic lay "beyond." Then came Columbus and the famous, gallant sail to the New World. One of our American poets has caught up the drama and the spirit of it in lines that stir the blood and lift the eyes to far horizons:

> *Behind him lay the grey Azores,*
> *Behind, the gates of Hercules;*

Before him not the ghost of shores,
  Before him only shoreless seas.
The good mate said, "Now we must pray,
  For lo! the very stars are gone,
Speak, admiral, what shall I say?"
  "Why, say 'Sail on! Sail on and on!'"

"My men grow mutinous day by day;
  My men grow ghastly, wan and weak."
The stout mate thought of home; a spray
  Of salt wave washed his swarthy cheek.
"What shall I say, brave admiral, say,
  If we sight naught but seas at dawn?"
"Why, we shall say at break of day,
  'Sail on! Sail on! Sail on and on!'"

They sailed and sailed as winds might blow
  Until at last the blanched mate said:
"Why, now not even God would know,
  Should I and all my men fall dead.
These very winds forget their way,
  For God from these dead seas is gone,
Now, speak, brave admiral, speak and say."
  He said, "Sail on! Sail on and on!"

They sailed. They sailed. Then spoke the mate:
  "This mad sea shows its teeth tonight.
He curls his lip, he lies in wait
  With lifted teeth as if to bite!
Brave admiral, say but one good word.
  What shall we do when hope is gone?"
The words leaped as a leaping sword,
  "Sail on! Sail on! Sail on and on!"

Then pale and worn he kept his deck,
  And peered through darkness. Ah, that night,
Of all dark nights! And then a speck—
  A light! A light! A light! A light!

It grew, a starlit flag, unfurled!
It grew to be Time's burst of dawn.
He gained a world, he gave the world
Its grandest lesson, "On and on."

II

And now observe how St. Paul's prayer moves purposefully into an area where we can call it a prayer for *light*. Immediately, however, we must warn ourselves against separating the asking for a growing love from the asking for a greatening light. There is a difference but it is a closely linked difference. The *Phillips* rendering brings this out: "My prayer for you is that you may have still more love—a love that is full of knowledge and wise insight."

Bishop Moule, in his *Philippian Studies,* combining translation with paraphrase, puts it thus: "that your love may abound yet more and more *in the attendant and protective blessing* of spiritual knowledge and all needed discernment."

Who was it, I wonder, who started the saying "Love is blind"? Whoever it was, it wasn't this man Paul. You are wrong, he says, in effect, if you fancy for a moment that this love which God has begun in you is an unregulated emotion or an unenlightened mysticism. It calls for, and seeks after, knowledge. Love, in the Christian sense, is a school, a curriculum, a discipline, with endless advances in the knowledge of Him who said, "Learn of me." Promotions there are, to be sure; but never any final diplomas.

The Apostle's strong word for knowledge—it's the ordinary Greek word plus the Pauline prefix that speaks of *thoroughness* and *fulness*—must be understood as being primarily a knowledge that is related to God's revelation in His Word and through His Son. It must be understood, further, as having to do with *life* and not merely with *theory*.

New Testament Christianity knows nothing of the philosopher's "ivory tower" where the attempt is made to achieve truth or to arrive at truth by "pure reason." From the Christian point of view, the reasoner himself is a sinner and, being a sinner, "private interest is always twisting truth to its own ends."

The knowledge that saves, says the New Testament, is the knowledge that comes by revelation and surrender. God has revealed Himself and His saving mercy not in a *lecture* but in a *life*—a life climaxed in a death and a resurrection. The truth about God and man and sin and salvation has not been *discussed*, it has been *done*. Our Lord's word is not, "I will show you the way and give you a lecture about truth and a treatise on life." No, His immensely saving word is: "I *am* the way, and the truth, and the life."

And, as a corollary of that word, He says: "If ye continue in my word, then are ye my disciples indeed; and ye shall know the truth, and the truth shall make you free" (John 8 : 32). Thus the Christian says, "If Christ is what we mean by life, if Christ is what we mean by truth, then I am committed to it, utterly and forever, be the price however great!"

In this surrender of love the dimensions of our knowledge will grow greater: in *depth,* for we shall get to know *ourselves* better; in *height,* for we shall get to know *God* better; in *length,* for we shall get to know *others* better.

And mark it well, please: all of this growing knowledge is founded, in one way or another, on the Holy Scriptures. Here is a revealing sentence that Hamilton Wright Mabie has written concerning our Abraham Lincoln and the Bible: "These sixty-six books emancipated him at once from the harsh and narrow conditions in which he was born; they set him in the great currents of human life; they brought before him the highest ideals of human character; and above all, for the purposes of education, they presented to his imagination the loftiest examples of human speech."[1]

The Christian lover who walks the way of excellency will ever pray:

[1] Walter Dudley Cavert, *Remember Now* (Abingdon-Cokesbury), p. 47.

Holy Spirit, Truth Divine,
Dawn upon this soul of mine;
Word of God, and inward Light,
Wake my spirit, clear my sight.

The prayer for light includes a second significant word: "judgment," as we have it in the Authorized Version. "Keen perception" is the Weymouth rendering. Moffatt makes it read: "all manner of insight."

It is a double-pronged word: subjectively, it may be taken to mean a kind of "sixth sense," a direct and penetrating intuition; objectively, it may be understood as a reference to the skill or wisdom with which love's captive makes use of the knowledge he possesses.

In the *Friend's Book of Discipline* we read: "Our power to perceive of the light of God is, of all our powers, the one which we need most to cultivate and develop. As exercise strengthens the body and education enlarges the mind, so the spiritual faculty within us grows as we use it in seeing and doing God's will." It is well said, provided its reference is to those who have passed under the quickening and sanctifying Lordship of Jesus Christ.

Let two observations suffice before we move on to a matter closely linked with this: (1) this way of excellency in love's discernment is the way of *listening*, and (2) the price of learning to listen is to *take time*. A woman who had been enormously and enthusiastically a woman of the world, now a child of faith and infectiously full of the Holy Spirit, wrote to a dear friend of mine:

"The Spirit is my check valve. I am so eager—eager to live, eager to learn, eager to go ahead, eager to love, eager to climb the ladder more than one step at a time! In all things the Spirit says to me: 'Thus far and no farther now!' Always the Spirit inspires, controls, and demands obedience. When I feel that driving, burning enthusiasm deep within, the Spirit never fails to remind me: 'Proceed with caution. Take time for all things; Rome was not built in a day.' God said to me, 'Mary, I have the whole universe to consider, not just you!' (My, how

deflating it was to hear that the first time!)" In these vivid
words one discovers how wholesome is the progress made even
by a young Christian in this area of discernment and understanding.

III

But come now to consider a third area of concern that St.
Paul enters as he prays for these Philippian Christians. We
must see his intercession as a prayer for *life*. Love grows in
the direction, and to the accompaniment, of knowledge. This
light of knowledge and discernment must, in turn, evidence
itself in our manner of conducting ourselves. Verses 10 and
11 now claim our attention. Here are four effects that follow
from an increase of love and light: (1) that you may "approve
things that are excellent"; (2) that you may "be sincere";
(3) that you may be "without offence"; and, (4) that you may
be "filled with the fruits of righteousness."

What a splendid quartet! Discriminativeness! Transparentness! Blamelessness! Fruitfulness!

Take the first. Because the Greek is somewhat ambiguous,
some scholars hold to the reading of the King James, "that
ye may approve things that are excellent," while others prefer
such a rendering as that of Adam Clark, "that ye put to
proof the things which differ." In the former rendering the
emphasis is on the thought of approval or approbation, whereas in the second translation the emphasis is on the testing
and differentiating. We need not tarry for argument about
the merits of either translation. Obviously, both ideas are in
the mind of the Apostle. The one involves the other. What is
the purpose of my discrimination if it is not to issue in giving
one thing a higher approval-rating than another? Or, to state
the matter conversely, how can I approve one thing as being
more excellent than another unless I exercise critical judgment? It is significant, I think, that the translators of the
Revised Standard Version have held very closely to the
translation of the Authorized Version. "Approve what is
excellent," is their rendering.

It all comes down to this: the Apostle wants these young Christians to understand that in the life of developing and deepening love there is a growing ability to appraise values and to make choices accordingly. Accompanying this ability is to be the steadfast disposition to select the best.

Have you taken a good look at this word "excellent?" Have you surveyed it as you would a soaring mountain peak? Unlike the word from which it springs—love—it has only one dimension, and that is *height*. It calls us up to the summits of living. It is not content when we merely leave the swamplands of low living, all malodorous and malarial. It is not even content when we top the foothills and look back upon the dismal depths from which we have ascended. It keeps saying, "Come up higher! Come up higher!"

Now what does this have to do with your every-day living and mine as Christians? Much, if I mistake not. You see the categories of experience within which our choices have to be made are not two but three. All of us know that there are things that are indecent, things that are decent, and things that are excellent. If we are even half-way under the government of the mind of Christ, we do not find it particularly difficult to choose between the indecent and the decent. What so often causes us to knit our brow and search our souls is the experience of being confronted by a choice between the decent and the excellent, the tolerable and the transcendent, the good and the best.

Well, there is no easy formula by which we can always and quickly determine what our choice will be. Still, we are leagues ahead if we commit ourselves to the best.

Apply this, for example, to your *reading*. Much of today's fiction has more in common with a cesspool than it does with a spring of water. There is so much of poison in it that Christian sensitiveness calls for just one kind of treatment—avoidance.

But when you have ruled out literary filth, you still have to deal with literary trash. It is the weakness of a great many of our books and magazines that they cater for nothing but the trivia of life. They remind me of a book review that I saw in the Literary Supplement of the *New York Times*. The reviewer of this particular volume of fiction said: "The trivial enthusiasms of the characters in this book make one feel that outright insanity would be intellectual promotion for them!"

While I am far from suggesting that literature in the lighter mood is to be kept clean away from the Christian's reading list, I could wish that something might be said to stimulate the masses of our church people today to furnish their minds and feed their souls with the things that are written by our finest authors. When did you last read a good biography? Are you making yourselves familiar with the devotional classics—treasures like the works of Fenelon, Thomas à Kempis, Lancelot Andrewes and John Woolman? Or, how long has it been since you worked up a bit of mental sweat over a fairly stiff volume in theology? It will do you no good to tell me that theological writings are too dull. Dull or not, a bracer in doctrine provides just the discipline that you need every now and again.

As for the volume that Walter Scott had in mind when he told his friend that "there is only one Book," do I need to tell you that not one of us has made himself its master and few of us are doing our Christian profession any credit by exploring it and exemplifying it with that insatiable diligence that it so richly deserves?

Or, take this commitment to the best and apply it to your *recreations*. An early church legend describes the aged Apostle John as going out now and again to play with a flock of doves, the little creatures fluttering about him and alighting from time to time on his shoulders and hands, while he talked to them as if they were his human friends. On one such occasion a hunter, happening along, expressed surprise that a man so pious as St. John would amuse himself by such an activity as this. St. John, pointing to the bow in the hunter's hand, asked him why he carried it with a loosened string. "Because," said the hunter, "it loses its strength unless it is given a chance to unbend." The dear old apostle, smiling, replied: "If even a piece of wood needs to unbend to retain its usefulness, why should you be surprised that a servant of Christ should sometimes relax and so keep himself stronger for his work?"

The point of this lovely legend I do not dispute for a moment. Piety that is overstrained is perilous piety.

But we live—you and I—in an age of amusement. We live in what Sorokin calls a "sensate culture"—a civilization that is much more concerned about pleasant emotions than it is about productive ideas. We live, moreover, in a culture that has taken recreation out of the hands of the people and put it in the hands of those who are commercially skilled to exploit it. The result is a sort of mob-mind that someone has described as "spectatoritis." We merely look on and get our play vicariously. This is not being disciples of what is excellent.

Each of us needs some hobby or recreation in which we are participant. Put some imagination into it. Be willing to learn something wholesome by means of it. Let it develop your mind and body skills. Don't be put off by the tendency to say, "Oh, well, I am not expert." Some games can relax and refresh you whether you are a champion or a duffer. When I play golf—which I greatly enjoy—I take comfort from G. K. Chesterton's remark that anything worth doing at all is worth doing badly!

But let's remember that if we are travellers on the road of excellency we shall see to it that our recreations are what the word says they should be: means by which we are re-created. If the game I play does not give a fine tang to life, making it easier for me to be a wholehearted follower of Christ, then I had better put in its place something that does.

But time says a stern "No" to our going on with these specific applications of the principle of excellency. Sometimes, in business or in politics, you may have to settle for the tolerably good, but don't live comfortably with it. Keep your fond eye on the superlatively good. The words that your own Tennyson puts on the lips of Queen Guinevere are worth recalling:

It was my duty to have loved the highest;
It surely was my profit had I known;
It would have been my pleasure had I seen.
We needs must love the highest when we see it,
*   Not Lancelot, nor another.*

This *discriminativeness*—with approval given to the best—
is one of the fine accompaniments that, according to St. Paul's
prayer, will be evident in the life of growing love and increasing light.

But there is another, which we shall call *transparentness*.
"That ye may be sincere," is the way the relevant clause
appears in the Authorized Version. Both Williams and
Weymouth render it, "that ye may be men of transparent
character." "That ye may be pure" is the way the Revised
Standard Version puts it.

The Greek word that is translated sincere means literally
"sun-tested" or "sun-judged." Among the ancients, we are
told, were slipshod sculptors who would produce statues from
blemished stone, filling the cracks with wax and painting
them over. But eventually the sun would peel the paint, melt
the wax, and reveal the cleverly covered ugliness. Without
wax! Free from sham, pretence, false fillings, complications!
"The idea of the Greek word," says Bishop Moule, "is that of
clearness, disengagement from complications." He observes
further that the Latin word from which our English "sincere"
is derived is the equivalent of our "unadulterated." It reminds
one of St. Paul's word in Romans 12 : 9, "let love be without
dissimulation," and elsewhere, you remember, the apostle
speaks of it as "love unfeigned."

The cynicism of many worldlings and the scepticism of
some theologians lead them to "doubt the possibility of pure
unselfish love in any human heart," as Dr. W. E. Sangster has
recently reminded us in his Cato Lectures. "Pierce to the
heart of it," say these cynics and sceptics, "and the grinning ego
still reigns." St. Paul would not have it so. He believed otherwise. He believed in the inward reign of the love of Christ

that gives freedom from the twist and tincture of deceit and doublemindedness. He would have rejoiced in the testimony of the Russian saint, Tikhon Zadonsky, who said: "Christ has loved me for nothing, and I must love Him for nothing too." Or in the witness of Sadhu Sundar Singh, the humble Indian exemplar of Christian sanctity, who said: "I have no desire for wealth, position or honour. Nor do I desire even heaven. But I do need Him Who has made my heart heaven."

Is there the painted wax of pretence in our lives? Are there false fillings of insecurity and sham? Is your Christian life fouled up with divided loyalties? If so, there is a stage along the trail of love's excellency which you have yet to reach. Won't you get down to business with God? Won't you let Him deeply and cleansingly fill you with His Holy Spirit? Remember that love's way is to be simple and utterly sincere —in motive, in attitude, in speech, in covenant, in making out reports, in all things.

The next accompaniment of deepening love and growing knowledge is *blamelessness*: "that ye may be . . . without offence."

On the face of it you might think that the reference is to our getting annoyed or piqued or insulted. While such an interpretation is not misleading so far as the facts are concerned, it does miss the precise point that St. Paul is making. "Without stumbling-block" is a more accurate rendering of the original. Scholars are agreed, I think, that, grammatically, the word may be taken either transitively or intransitively. If we interpret it transitively it means that the love-impelled Christian does not have in him that which causes others to stumble. If we take it intransitively, we understand St. Paul to mean that we do not experience stumbling, do not allow obstacles to "throw" us and defeat us.

Tyndale and Cranmer translate the whole clause so as to make it read, "that ye may be pure and such as [should] hurt no man's conscience."

The Indian philosopher, Bara Dada, brother of Rabindranath Tagore, once said: "Jesus is ideal and wonderful, but

you Christians—you are not like Him." According to those
who reported the incident, it was not said bitterly but sadly.
Had those Christians, by their unlovely and unloving ways,
put a stumbling-block in the path of the kindly old philosopher who might have been won to the Master?

On the other hand, one thinks of the conversion of Dr.
Kagawa of Japan. Disagree with some of his view if you will,
but still you are obliged to recognize this selfless leader's passionate devotion to Christ and His Kingdom. In his home
town there once toiled a missionary by the name of Logan.
Years later, someone said to Dr. Kagawa, "Do you know Dr.
Logan?" Smilingly he replied: "He was the first one who
showed me the blueprint of love." It was Logan who led
Kagawa to Christ. No "occasion of stumbling" there!

Perfect love does not insure perfect practice. It would be a
mistake for me to imply that it does. What *may* be insured
is a perfect purpose; and in the perfection of that holy purpose,
constantly renewed by the Holy Spirit, the practice will be
constantly corrected upward.

Accordingly, we hear St. Paul urging these Philippian
Christians: "work out your own salvation with fear and
trembling. For it is God which worketh in you both to will
and to do of his good pleasure. Do all things without murmur-
ings and disputings." Why? "That ye may be blameless and
harmless, the sons of God, without rebuke, in the midst of a
crooked and perverse nation, among whom ye shine as lights
in the world" (ch. 2: 12–15).

Discriminativeness, transparentness, blamelessness—and
now one thing more: *fruitfulness.* Verse 11 puts it beautifully,
"Being filled with the fruits of righteousness, which are by
Jesus Christ, unto the glory and praise of God."

St. Paul is not content, even as God is not, with lives that
are negatively good—free from "offence"; he prays for lives
that are positively good—laden with the "fruits of righteousness." In the days when I was growing up in Southern
California, where the citrus fruit industry is so important a
part of the economy, I learned that a tree can be so "budded"

as to produce an astonishing variety of fruits. The tree of love, which is indeed the tree of righteousness, is one tree, but the heavenly Horticulturalist has caused it to bear fruit that is rich and varied. There is "joy." There is "peace." There is "long-suffering." There is "gentleness." There are "goodness," "faith," "meekness," and "temperance." And these are not occasionals or seasonals; they are perennials! They are to go on bearing fruit "till the day of Christ" (v. 10).

We must conclude. Love's way of excellency has had our attention. Does it have also our allegiance? Whenever it does, whether in the first century or the twentieth, the love-filled life bears its own singular Christian fruitage.

Do you remember the story of Phocas, the Gardener Saint of Asia Minor? Belonging to the fourth century, he lived in a little cottage outside the city gate of Sinope. Travellers passed his door almost all hours of the day and night. By the holy ingenuity of love he stopped as many of them as possible. Were they not weary? Let them rest themselves, sitting in his well-tended garden. Were they in need of a friendly word? He would speak it to them—in the dear Master's name.

But then, quite suddenly one day, life was all changed for Phocas. Orders went out from Emperor Diocletian that the Christians must be put out of business. When the persecutors entered Sinope, they were under orders to find a man by the name of Phocas and put him to death. About to enter the city one hot afternoon, they passed in front of the old man's cottage and garden. In his innocence he treated them as though they were his warmest friends, begging them to pause a while and rest themselves. They consented. So warm and gracious was the hospitality they received that when their host invited them to stay the night and go on their way refreshed next day, they agreed to do so.

"And what *is* your business?" said Phocas, unsuspectingly.

They then told him that they would answer his question if he would regard it as a secret. It was obvious to them by now that he was a man to be trusted. Who were they? Why, they were the lictors of Rome, searching for a certain "Phocas,"

who was a Christian. And please, if their kind host knew him
would he be so good as to help them to identify him. After
all, he was a dangerous follower of this Jesus about whom the
Christians talked, and he must be executed immediately.

"I know him well," said Phocas quietly. "He is quite near.
. . . Let us attend to it in the morning."

His guests having retired, Phocas sat thinking. Escape?
That would be easy. He had only to leave under cover of
darkness. At daybreak he could be at least twenty miles away.
He knew fellow Christians who would give him hospitality
by hiding him. When the persecution had passed, he could
reappear and once again cultivate his garden.

The decision to flee into safety or to stay unto death was
apparently made without struggle or delay. Out into his
garden Phocas went and began digging. Was there any
earthly thing he loved better than this little plot of ground
—the odour of the humus, the "feel" of the soil, the miracle
of fertility. What were his thoughts as he went on digging?

There was still time to run away. But the Saviour did not
run—neither from His Gethsemane nor His Calvary. Or,
perhaps he thought of his fellow Christians to whom he might
go for asylum. Would not his coming endanger them? As
for these executioners that now were soundly sleeping under
his roof, they were, after all, only men who were carrying out
orders. If they failed to find their man, their own lives, likely
as not, would be taken.

Deeper and deeper Phocas dug. Before dawn he was done.
There it was—his own grave.

Morning came, and with it the waking of the executioners.
"I am Phocas," he said calmly. We have it on the word of the
Christian bishop who recorded the story for posterity, that
the men stood "motionless" in astonishment. They couldn't
believe it! And when they did believe it, they obviously were
reluctant to perform an execution without mercy on a man
who had shown them nothing but mercy.

It was the persuasion of Phocas himself that overcame their
reluctance. They had a duty to perform. He knew it. He was

not bitter at them. Besides, death did not terrify him, he assured them. Toward them he bore nothing but the love of Christ.

Moments later it was all over. The sword had done its work. And the body of Christ's love-mastered man lay in the stillness of death in the garden he loved so dearly.

My dear friends, the fruitfulness of a life like that is as far beyond our ability to measure it as it is beyond the power of words to describe it.

Only when the "day of Christ" comes will we see it in its perfect fruition. What a day that will be! Our day? Yes. But supremely—His day! "Behold he cometh with clouds, and every eye shall see him" (Revelation 1 : 7). About His person shall be wrapped those glittering garments that dazzled the apostolic trio on the Transfiguration Mount. Above His throne the emerald rainbow shall circle. Around Him shall be gathered the millions who form the bride of His heart— the wondering, worshipping, transfigured subjects of His Calvary passion. They are His "jewels," His "peculiar treasure!" He loved them; they loved Him. Now they are His crown. Not gold of Ophir, or diamonds of Kimberly, or pearls of Ceylon—not gems so tawdry as these—but the souls of men by blood redeemed!

Hark! Do you hear that? It is the million-throated bursting of such a doxology as earth has never heard: "Unto him that loved us, and washed us from our sins in his own blood, and hath made us kings and priests unto God and his Father; to him be glory and dominion forever and ever. Amen."

It is the consummation of the way of excellency. It is "the day of Christ!"

PRAYER AND THE WAY OF CONSISTENCY

"For this cause we also, since the day we heard it, do not cease to pray for you, and to desire that ye might be filled with the knowledge of his will in all wisdom and spiritual understanding; That ye might walk worthy of the Lord unto all pleasing, being fruitful in every good work, and increasing in the knowledge of God; Strengthened with all might, according to his glorious power, unto all patience and longsuffering with joyfulness; Giving thanks unto the Father, which hath made us meet to be partakers of the inheritance of the saints in the light." Colossians 1: 9–12.

"For I would that ye knew what great conflict I have for you, and for them at Laodicea, and for as many as have not seen my face in the flesh; That their hearts might be comforted, being knit together in love, and unto all riches of the full assurance of understanding, to the acknowledgment of the mystery of God, and of the Father, and of Christ." Colossians 2: 1–2.

III

PRAYER AND THE WAY OF CONSISTENCY

ST. PAUL is our highest and best representative of what
someone has called "the Apostolate of Intercession." As
such, he shows us in his Colossian prayer how necessary
it is to link Christian piety with Christian practice. We are
going to see that the central burden of this prayer is disclosed
in the words of verse 10: "That ye might walk worthy of the
Lord unto all pleasing." This is the core of consistency apart
from which discipleship has no convincing firmness.

This consistency is easily missed—always with unhappy
consequences. When it is lacking, moreover, we always
recognize it in our really lucid moments. One hears Francis
Bacon saying, "I have taken all knowledge for my province;
but, alas, I have not taken all virtue for my practice." Or one
recalls what Bobby Burns wrote to a friend on a New Year's
Day: "This, Dear Madam, is a morning of wishes: and would
to God that I came under the Apostle James' description:
'The effectual, fervent prayer of a *righteous man* availeth
much.' In that case, Madam, you would welcome in a year
full of blessings." The pathetic Ayrshire poet knew, with sure
instinct, that corrupt character turns the edge of prayer.

We want none of this, says St. Paul, as he unveils his
praying soul to the Christians in Colossae. More important,
Christ wants none of this. Hence my prayer in your behalf.

I

Consider the *occasion* of this prayer. Attention to it is
proper enough since the apostle introduces the prayer by
saying, "For this cause . . ." (v. 9).

53

We have no evidence that St. Paul had ever visited the community of believers at Colossae, an Asia Minor town approximately a hundred miles inland from Ephesus. About the year 62, while he was a prisoner in Rome, he received a visit from Epaphras, who was in all probability the church's founder and pastor. It was a mixed report that Epaphras brought. Parts of it kindled a light in St. Paul's eyes. Parts of it produced a heavy sigh of concern. All in all, it was felt that a letter must be dispatched to the Christians there. It was written, and off it went by the hand of Tychicus.

With the text of the letter before us we can say that the occasion of it has both *background* and *foreground*. Wisely, tactfully, graciously, St. Paul waits a bit, in his writing, before he deals with matters that are distressing to him and dangerous to them. From this background he begins to draw out his strong words of concern and correction in chapter 2, which opens with the statement, "I wish you could understand how deep is my anxiety for you" (Phillips).

Meanwhile, he has thrust into the foreground of his reason for writing them not less than three considerations that have brought immense gladness to his spirit. "We give thanks to God and the Father of our Lord Jesus Christ, praying always for you, since we heard (1) of your faith in Christ Jesus, and (2) of the love which ye have to all the saints, and (3) for the hope which is laid up for you in heaven" (v. 3–5).

1. Through *faith* you are linked with Christ. "Faith," says Matthew Henry, "opens the door of the soul to receive Christ; faith admits Him, and submits to Him." All this is true, but it is not the whole truth of what Paul is saying here. In many passages in the New Testament saving faith is described by means of a Greek preposition that means, literally, "*into* Christ." It describes *action toward* and *arrival at*, if you will allow the awkwardness. John 3: 16 might be so read, for example: "that whosoever believeth *into* Christ."

But in several passages, this being one of them, Paul employs the Greek preposition that means, quite literally, "in" rather than "into." "Into" makes Christ the *object* of our faith, whereas "in" makes Him the *element* and *atmosphere* of our faith. It is as though the Apostle were saying to these Christians: Your trust not only looks *to* Christ, as the One Who by His death has redeemed you to God; it rests *in* Christ, as the one Who by His Spirit lives in you—and you in Him.

2. In *love* they are linked with one another. This is a further reason for the grateful concern that St. Paul feels for these Christians whom he has never seen. It does me good, says the Apostle, to hear of "the love which ye have to all the saints," or "all God's people," as Goodspeed and Williams translate it. In Christian circles love, of course, is everybody's word. Perhaps that's the trouble: it's just a word—a verbalism instead of a verity. Some Christians are not in love with people; they are just in love with love. They remind one of the man who said, "I love *humanity,* but I don't like *people.*"

The famous Kansas psychiatrist, Dr. Karl Menninger, was asked at a forum what he would do if he felt a nervous breakdown coming on. Perhaps the questioner expected him to say, "I would go to a psychiatrist." If so, he was disappointed. What Menninger said was, "If you feel a nervous breakdown coming on, lock up your house, go across the railway tracks and find someone in need and do something for him." What lies beneath that advice is clear enough, is it not? Most cases of nervous distress grow out of preoccupation with ourselves. The cure for that is the love of Christ that, because of its warm affection toward Him, carries us out of ourselves in a solicitous ministry to others.

"Behold how these Christians love one another!" was the exclamation of one who watched the conduct of the early disciples. Undoubtedly it was the cohesive power and the superlative beauty of this love that made Diognetus say in his ancient "Epistle": "What the soul is to the body, so the Christians are to the world. They hold the world together."

3. And then by *hope* these Colossians were linked with heaven. This completes the famous and familiar Pauline triad of *faith, love,* and *hope.* The reference to "the hope which is laid up for you in heaven" is cast in a form that

makes it notable. It is not precisely parallel in construction to the "faith" phrase and the "love" phrase. The syntax is such as to suggest that hope not only comes on as a natural climax toward which faith and love point, but it actually kindles and inspires and enhances the faith and the love.

By saying that hope links these believers to heaven I do not mean a restricted view of heaven, as the eternal abode of the righteous. I mean rather what the Apostle means elsewhere when he speaks of the coming again *from heaven* of our Lord Jesus Christ. Weymouth's translation of Philippians 3 : 20, 21 is lucid and excellent. "We, however, are free citizens of heaven, and we are waiting with long expectation for the coming from heaven of a Saviour, the Lord Jesus Christ, who, in the exercise of the power which he has even to subject all things to himself, will transform this body of our humiliation until it resembles the body of his glory."

We should try to grasp what is really important here. The hope of the Christian looks ahead to the return and the reign of Christ. God has decreed it. God will bring it to pass. Thus the Christian hope is not man-generated; it is God-given. It is such that the human mind, no matter how resolute its fibre, could neither contrive it nor sustain it. A naturally optimistic temperament could not produce it. Upon the contrary, it is positioned on what God *is* in His eternal purpose, and what He has *done* in Christ, and on what He *will do* "when he shall come to be glorified in his saints, and to be admired in all them that believe . . . in that day" (2 Thessalonians 1 : 10).

Now the question might well arise, If Paul is led to thankful prayer because he has learned of the faith, love, and hope of these Colossians, how does it come to pass that his prayer is fraught with burden and passionate anxiety? He has not gone far with his letter until he says, "I wish you could understand how deep is my anxiety for you" (ch. 2 : 1, Phillips).

The explanation, of course, lies in the threat to these Christians of the so-called "Colossian heresy." Nowhere in the epistle does St. Paul give us a formal description of it. Repeatedly, nevertheless, he alludes to it. Take, for example, the 8th verse of chapter 2: "Be careful that nobody spoils your faith, through intellectualism or high-sounding nonsense. Such stuff is at best founded on men's ideas of the nature of the world and disregards Christ" (Phillips).

Scholars are generally agreed that the heretical poison of which St. Paul speaks so vehemently was a mixture of at least three strains: (1) budding Gnosticism, (2) Judaism, and (3) asceticism. Part of the *gnosis*—the illumination of the initiated—consisted of the philosophy that matter is inherently evil and that God could not therefore have been its Creator. Hence God was pictured as removed from the material creation by a series of demigods. Among these superior powers, as distinguished from the Supreme Power, was Christ.

It is not difficult to understand how that heresy inflamed the soul of St. Paul, believing as he did so uncompromisingly in the full deity and eternal glory of Jesus Christ. Christ is not one among many, or one among a few, cries this titan of a Christian! He is "the exact likeness of the unseen God, His first-born Son who existed before any created thing" (v. 15, Williams). God has ordained it that "all the divine fulness should dwell in Him, and that through Him He might reconcile to Himself all things on earth or in heaven, making this peace through the blood He shed on His cross" (v. 19, Williams).

It is fatal to your faith, Paul insists, to be carried away from this superlative view of the person and ministry of the Lord Jesus Christ. It is, moreover, futile to abandon this true conception of our Lord for banal speculations and man-centred asceticisms.

Hold to Christ! Hold to Christ! I cannot pray a lesser prayer for you.

> *None other Lamb, none other Name,*
> *None other hope in heaven, or earth, or sea,*
> *None other hiding place from guilt and shame,*
> *None beside Thee.*

When I think of your "faith," "love," and "hope," says
Paul, I pray for you with delight. But when I think of the
fanciful theories and the enslaving legalisms that are being
offered you, whose effect can be none other than to corrupt
your faith, narrow your love, and dim your hope, then I
pray for you with distress. There's an unnameable "conflict"
(2 : 1) in my heart over you, for I want you to "continue in
the faith grounded and settled, and be not moved away from
the hope of the gospel" (1 : 23).

It is this emotional blend of delight and distress that gives
rise to the prayer whose central burden must next have our
attention.

II

Consider the *objective* of the apostle's intercession for the
Colossians. It is stated in the finely chiselled and enormously
challenging words of verse 10: "That ye might walk worthy
of the Lord unto all pleasing . . ."

In some of the later translations there are values of clarifi-
cation and enrichment that we should not miss. Goodspeed
renders it: "that the lives you live may be worthy of your
Master, and wholly pleasing to Him." Arthur Way has it:
"that you may pass through life in a manner worthy of our
Lord, so as to please Him entirely." Moffatt makes it read:
"that you may lead a life that is worthy of the Lord and
give Him entire satisfaction."

Four things emerge here:

1. Something *practical*: "that ye might walk." This con-
cerns, as Phillips brings out, "your outward lives, which men
see." If discipleship isn't demonstrated, it is devastated. If
Christian holiness isn't ethical, it is empty.

Dr. Harold Cooke Phillips, in his "Yale Lectures," recalls
a story that his mother told about a very pious grocer whose
living quarters were above his place of business. Of a morning
he was known to call down to his young clerk and say:
"James."

"Yes, sir."

"Have you watered the milk?"

"Yes, sir."

"Have you pumpkined the butter?"

"Yes, sir."

"And put chicory in the coffee?"

"Yes, sir."

"Then come up to worship!"

Piety divorced from practice! It's worse than a pity; it's a travesty. Over against it is the example of the missionary concerning whom one of the observant nationals said: "He walks as he talks!" Such was the witness for which Paul was praying.

2. Something *congenial*: "that ye might walk worthy of the Lord." The suggestion is not that of *merit* but of *fitness*. Yours is to be a behaviour, says the Apostle, that is appropriate to the Saviour you trust and the Lord you follow. When Dannecker was asked by Napoleon to do a statue of Venus, he declined. Pressed by the insistent Napoleon, he finally said, to explain his refusal, "My chisel has done Jesus Christ and it can never be lowered to do a Greek goddess!"

Christians never walk the highway of great living until they reach the place where, entirely apart from specific commands or prohibitions of Scripture, they are concerned chiefly about the clear congeniality of certain modes of behaviour and the sheer inappropriateness of others. It was this lofty control over conduct to which Dannecker was bending.

"Worthy!" It is a fine word. Paul was fond of it. He exhorts the Ephesians, "walk worthy of the vocation wherewith ye are called" (4: 1). He urges the Philippians, "let your manner of life be worthy of the gospel" (1: 27, RSV). His longing for the Thessalonians is that they "would walk worthy of God" (I, 2: 12). And here, in the Colossian epistle, he pleads for something that, in a sense, is the climax of all, namely, that these Christian brothers and sisters might "walk worthy of the Lord" Jesus Christ, the Lord of glory.

3. Something *crucial*: "that ye might set out walking." This amplified rendering is suggested by Handley Moule in his

Colossian Studies. He gives it this turn, he explains, in an attempt to bring out the force of the aorist tense in which the word "walk" appears. The effect of this rendering, says Moule, is to make us think of Paul's prayer as envisaging "a new departure" in the Christian's walk.

This insight of Moule's reminded me of a sermon by J. Gregory Mantle on the familiar text, "And Enoch walked with God" (Genesis 5: 24). Mantle speaks of the "crisis hour in an already Christian life" such as has come to so many of God's children. The previous walk has been a mixture of God-reliance and self-sufficiency: now the self-sufficiency is shattered. The previous walk has had its haltings, not to say its wanderings: now it is given an undaunted steadiness.

Dr. Mantle drew for illustration from the life of Mr. Moody. There was the crisis in the beloved evangelist's life that came shortly after the Chicago fire, in which both Church and Institute had been destroyed. He was in New York City, soliciting funds for the rebuilding project. The notable thing that took place is best told, Mantle rightly feels, in Moody's own words:

> "My heart was not in the work of begging. I could not appeal for money. I was crying all the time that God would fill me with His Spirit. One day in the city of New York— Oh, what a day! I cannot describe it. I seldom refer to it. It is almost too sacred an experience to name. Paul had an experience of which he never spoke for fourteen years. I can only say that God revealed Himself to me, and I had such an experience of His love that I had to ask Him to stay His hand. When I began preaching again my sermons were not different. I did not present any new truths, yet hundreds were converted. I would not go back to where I was before that blessed experience if you should give me all the world."

On which Dr. Mantle makes the terse comment: "Dwight Lyman Moody henceforth walked with God." Something crucial had occurred to make it so.

4. Something *evangelical*: "unto all pleasing." The English translation is improved in such renderings as that of Moffatt: to "give him [the Lord] entire satisfaction." Weymouth makes it read: "perfectly pleasing to him."

Why do I speak of this as something "evangelical?" Because I want you to see it as part of the "good news" of Christ our Lord. Held out before us here is nothing short of a disposition, a spirit, a temper, which, whatever others may say about it, is pleasing to God.

The Greek word for "unto all pleasing" is of special interest to the scholars, and this for two reasons. For one thing, it occurs nowhere else in the New Testament. In addition, it is an illustration of how the Holy Spirit leads an inspired Christian writer to lay hold of a word which, in classical Greek, has an unfavourable and uncomplimentary meaning which, nevertheless, by the Spirit's use of it. is redeemed to a meaning fine and enviable. In its bad sense it is descriptive of a person who is obsequious, spinelessly subservient. But as St. Paul employs the word, it describes the Christian of sensitive sanctity whose constant eagerness is for "all meeting of His wishes," to use the translation of Handley Moule.

If there is a whole battery of perfectionisms that we dare not be drawn into because of our loyalty to the Scriptures, let's be sure we do not miss the one unassailable perfectionism that grace provides and the Scriptures disclose. Not *absolute* perfection: that were fantastic. Not *legal* perfection: that were to return to the law and to retreat from grace. Not *service* perfection: that were to overlook obvious awkwardness and clumsiness. Not *behavioral* perfection: that were to fly in the face of a hundred flaws in our manners. Not *sinless* perfection: that were to imply a status identical with our "unfallen" Lord.

What then? Let's call it *affectional* and *dispositional* perfection. It is God's own gift to totally committed children of His, who, renouncing self-pleasing and men-pleasing, are imbued with a passionate eagerness to please Him in all things. True. St. Paul would have each of us "please his

neighbour" if he can (Romans 15: 2), but if he can't, his in-
flexible aim must be to please God.

It is further true that "they that are in the flesh cannot
please God" (Romans 8: 8). Yet it is equally true that "ye
are not in the flesh, but in the Spirit, if so be that the Spirit
of God dwell in you" (8: 9).

If you want an inspiring exercise, compare 1 Thessalonians
4: 1 with Hebrews 11: 5. In the one you read, "ye ought to
walk and to please God." In the other you read of Enoch,
who, as we have already noted "walked with God," that he
had "this testimony, that he pleased God." One is exhortation;
the other is exhibition. To hear it in a *plea* is challenging;
to see it in a *picture* is heartening.

Bishop Lester Smith of Ohio tells a delightful story about
a college Commencement in Missouri at which he was the
speaker. Among the graduates was a farmer boy who plainly
was from a poor home. He wore blue jeans, a blue chambray
shirt and a coat with patched sleeves. There came that tense
moment when the scholarship award was to be given to the
unknown student who stood first in his grades. The sealed
envelope containing the name of the winner and the medal
which was to be awarded was opened. When the name was
read it proved to be that of the farmer boy. The applause
died away, the exercises were concluded, and the recessional
begun.

Bishop Smith said that he fell in line behind the boy. They
came down the aisle to a point where there sat a man with
a heavy beard not too closely shaven and a suit of clothes that
looked as if it had never seen the presser. Next to him sat a
little lady in a gingham dress and a sunbonnet. The lad
stopped, dropped the medal in his mother's lap, and pressed
a kiss against her cheek. As he withdrew, the bishop saw the
little mother reach over a small hand and put it around the
fingers of her husband's big callous hand and squeeze it, as,
looking up into his face, she said, "It's worth all it cost, isn't
it?" They beamed upon each other like eighteen-year-old
lovers. Their son was a pleasure to them!

Well, somewhere I have read of a people concerning whom it is said that "God is not ashamed to be called their God." They must have been a pleasure to Him.

This—and nothing less—was the *objective* that had shaped itself in Paul's heart as he prayed for the Colossians. A noble and not unattainable objective it was: "that ye might walk worthy of the Lord unto all pleasing."

III

Consider next the *order* of the prayer. Something goes *before* and something comes *after* this clause of purpose which we have been examining, and the relationships are significant.

See what precedes: I "do not cease to pray for you, and to desire that ye might be filled with the knowledge of his will in all wisdom and spiritual understanding" (v. 9).

See what follows: "being fruitful in every good work, and increasing in the knowledge of God; strengthened with all might, according to his glorious power, unto all patience and longsuffering with joyfulness" (v. 10, 11).

Now from these portions of the prayer we may deduce at least three major values:

1. For one thing, it is clear that if we are to live God-pleasing lives, we must have *enlightenment with respect to God's will.*

The Apostle's language is strong, and for good reason. It appears that the peddlers of the "Colossian heresy" made a great deal of the *pleroma*, the "fulness." Be initiated, they said, into this understanding of the emanations, the demigods, the "elemental powers," and you will have the "fulness" of knowledge.

Not so, cries Paul! These are profitless speculations. Don't be taken in by them! What you need is something much simpler, much more practical, and much more humbling: you need a "thorough knowledge" (the Greek word translated "knowledge" requires the adjective!) of God's *will.*

It is as untrue as it is unfair to say that New Testament Christianity is anti-intellectual. The Gospel allows the full

play of truth—all truth—upon the mind. What *is* fair to say
—and it is what Greek intellectualism has always found
difficult to swallow—is that Christianity is less interested in
what Kant called "pure reason," or the speculative play of the
intellect, than it is in what he called "practical reason," or
moral earnestness and wholeness.

Here, in intercession, Paul seems to say, Brothers, you can't
know all the mystery of God's *nature* or of God's *providence*,
but you can know the essentials of His *will* for you. Let your
will come to terms with His. Be committed to it. Else life
for you will run in circles until you drop from exhaustion and
futility.

Paul was, of course, in agreement with his Lord who said,
"If any man will to do his will, he shall know of the doctrine,
whether it be of God, or whether I speak of myself" (John
7 : 17). And the famous Robertson of Brighton was in agreement both with Jesus and Paul when he preached his
celebrated sermon on "Obedience as the Organ of Knowledge."

Two college chaps of Christian profession were in convers-
ation. One said to the other, "I wish I knew what God wanted
me to do in life." Said his mate, "Have you prayed about it?"
"Yes." "No answer?" "No." "Were you sincere?" "I think
so. Of course, there are one or two things I don't want Him
to ask me to do, for I wouldn't do them."

Do we call that prayer? It is closer to a mild blasphemy.
Do we call that surrender? It is an unworthy piece of bargain-
ing. Do we call that the seeking of God's will? It is a not too
pious form of evasion.

On the other hand, when we are open to God's will, in
sympathy with it, dedicated to it, the light comes through.
Here we see the significance of the phrase, "In all spiritual
wisdom and understanding." One is entitled to doubt the
validity of too nice a play on the words "wisdom" and "understanding." In their classical Greek meaning "wisdom" may
well signify the ability to grasp first principles, such as those
which belong to a particular art or craft, and "understanding"
may signify the critical facility that one develops under

another's tutorship. That these shadings are in Paul's mind at the moment of his writing is doubtful. His purpose is practical, not philosophical or theoretical.

I cannot forget a comment on the expression "spiritual understanding" which I heard many years ago from the lips of an Irish Methodist who drank deeply at the fountain of Holy Scripture. He told us that he liked to think that this phrase meant "an understanding of spiritual things and a spiritual understanding of other things." It is the light of Christ's mind playing over every phase and feature of our lives and relating them to the will of God. Where there are issues—social, economic, industrial, political, vocational—on which the Father's will is obscure to us, there we walk softly in the half-light, claiming His mercy for our dulness, eager always for further light to break.

Many of you will have read the strangely haunting hymn whose words were written by Madame Guyon in the midst of one of her many periods of imprisonment and pain through which she passed 250 years ago. The physical disfigurement that came to this woman of noble birth and extraordinary beauty did not mar the elegance of her spirit. Because, whether in prison or out, the will of God was for her supreme, she was able to write:

> *A little bird I am*
> *Shut from the field of air;*
> *Yet in my cage I sit and sing*
> *To Him who placed me there;*
> *Well pleased a prisoner to be,*
> *Because, my God, it pleases Thee.*
>
> *Nought have I else to do;*
> *I sing the whole day long;*
> *And He whom most I love to please,*
> *Doth listen to my song;*
> *He caught and bound my wandering wing*
> *But still He bends to hear me sing.*

E

My cage confines me round;
  Abroad I cannot fly;
But though my wing is closely bound,
  My heart's at liberty.
My prison walls cannot control
The flight, the freedom of the soul.

Oh! it is good to soar
  These bolts and bars above,
To Him whose purpose I adore,
  Whose Providence I love;
And in Thy mighty will to find
The joy, the freedom of the mind.

2. Come now to the second value that arises as we study
the order of this prayer. Prerequisite to consistent living—
the walking "worthy of the Lord unto all pleasing"—there
is, as we have seen, an enlightenment regarding God's will.
Next we learn that in this walk there is *an enhancement in
God's work*: "being fruitful in every good work and increasing in the knowledge of God" (v. 10).

I shall assume the correctness of the view that the two
participles, "bearing fruit" and "increasing" (which is the
translation of the RSV) are to be taken together and that both
are modified by the words "in every good work." That is to
say, "in every good work" we are both to bear "fruit" and to
increase "in the knowledge of God."

In verse 6 Paul uses the same form of address to describe,
impersonally, the effect of the Gospel in the world. The
Gospel is "bearing fruit and growing," says the RSV. Now,
in verse 10, Paul makes the same thought personal: *you* are
to be "bearing fruit and growing."

The emphasis upon "you" is deserving of a moment's notice.
The fruitfulness *of* our service is not so much in the Apostle's
mind as *our* fruitfulness *in* the service. What is more, the
knowledge of God's will, at which we looked, is not so much
to the fore as the knowledge of God *Himself*.

Take the pioneer missionaries who were the trailblazers in world evangelism a century ago. Some of them, like the Moffatts and the Morrisons, went for years before they witnessed a single conversion among the pagan people to which they preached. Was theirs a stagnant, sterile life? Perish the thought! In them the fragrant graces that Paul calls "the fruit of the Spirit" were ripening. In them the intimacies which are possible between a redeemed soul and God were growing richer. In them a faith, which, to be sure, was sometimes drastically tested, was sinking deeper roots.

Or, to take a quite different experience, I think of the moving witness that is given by an American preacher, Dr. Albert Day, in his book called *An Autobiography of Prayer*. Time was, says Dr. Day, when prayer to be helped in sermon preparation was almost entirely devoid of the discipline of quiet "listening." In those days sermon research and writing were something of an "agony," he confesses. Then he learned the art of listening, and all was changed. His own words are best:

"Therefore, without abating my own diligence in reading and study and meditation, I would look expectantly to Him, to take all of my mental and spiritual efforts and illuminate and guide them into the truth He wanted my people to hear, and to add the creative touch which would make of scattered truths and miscellaneous insights a living and convincing unity of ideas. So sermonic labour for God became spirit-listening to God. After that, the task became a joy. Sermons were still far from what I wanted them to be . . . They still are! But at least something was given to me—and increasingly through the years."[1]

Will any of us say that this was not enhancement in God's work? Especially when we remember that "enhancement" comes to us through the Old French in a word that means to "raise," to "add to," to "make greater!"

[1] Albert E. Day, *An Autobiography of Prayer* (New York: Harper & Brothers), p. 29.

Help us, O Lord, that we may grow
In grace as Thou dost grace bestow;
And still Thy richer gifts repeat
Till grace in glory is complete.

3. In the orderly sequence of this prayer we come next to the words, "Strengthened with all might, according to his glorious power, unto all patience and longsuffering with joyfulness." This carries us beyond enlightenment on God's will and enhancement in God's work. Here is *empowerment along God's way.*

Is there someone who takes seriously this call to consistency? Is there someone who catches the Apostle's insight into the necessary Christian connection between *knowledge* and *obedience*, between *doctrine* and *duty*? Is it, perchance, someone who says, Yes, the Christian logic of all this I admit, but *how* can I carry it out? The reach of it exceeds my grasp. The weight of it is heavier than I can carry.

Ah, yes, says Paul, that I understand well. But my prayer for you includes the gift of power that will enable you to "walk worthy of the Lord unto all pleasing."

And what power!

Think of the *proportion* in which this power is offered. I want to put two alternative translations together here because each is excellent in its way: "strengthened with strength of every kind" (Weymouth), "according to the might of His glory" (Moule).

The "might of His glory" in *creation* is no mean thing, but this is not our measuring line. The "might of His glory" in *providence* is no meagre affair, but this is not our measure. No, the measure and model of the power offered us through His Holy Spirit are to be seen in the glory of His Cross, Resurrection, and Ascension. You have thrilled—have you not?—to that glowing word of Paul's in the opening of the letter to the Romans. The RSV rendering is superior: Jesus "was descended from David according to the flesh and designated Son of God in power, according to the Spirit of holiness by his resurrection from the dead" (1: 3, 4).

Samuel Chadwick of Cliff used to insist that just as the crossing of the Red Sea became the "standard miracle" of the Old Testament, so the Resurrection of our Lord became the standard miracle of the New. Christ's utter rout of His foes was made the measure and the guarantee of the conquest *we* may know through Him.

If only we realized this! In recent months one of our large petrol companies in America has been publishing a series of advertisements in which they have shown, for example, the Empire State Building lifted from its foundation into the air, the explanation being that there is enough power, if fully released, in one gallon of the petrol produced by this company to raise the colossal skyscraper a measured number of inches.

But there's the rub—"if fully released!" The late Dr. A. B. Simpson, founder of the Christian and Missionary Alliance, speaking of his crisis of the deeper life, said: "The Lord Jesus revealed Himself as a living and all-sufficient presence, and I learned for the first time that Christ had not saved us from future peril, and left us to fight the battle of life as best we could; but He who had justified us was waiting to sanctify us, to enter into our spirit, and substitute His strength, His holiness, His joy, His love, His faith, His power, for all our worthlessness, helplessness and nothingness, and make it an actual living fact."

Thus began, in a high hour of vision and cleansing and enduement, a new realization of the potent adequacy of the risen, regnant Christ.

And now a word about the *purpose,* as well as the proportion, of this power. Here, I suspect, the first-time reader of Paul's prayer would be pulled up with surprise. "Strengthened with all might, according to his glorious power, *unto* . . ." What? Surely the offer of such immense resources would carry with it the purpose of, let us say, enabling us to preach a mighty sermon like John Livingstone's at Shotts, or start a nation-wide revival as did John Wesley in the eighteenth century, or head up a new movement in missions as did Hudson Taylor in the China Inland Mission. No! Nothing of the sort is mentioned by this princely intercessor.

Instead, he informs us that "the great moral purpose" of our being so mightily endued is that we may have and exhibit "all patience and longsuffering." "Unlimited patience and perseverance" is the translation of the Berkeley Version.

We must see that in the abundant life of Christ's indwelling fulness, through the Holy Spirit, there are two ranges of power. One is related to the *active* side of the Christian's— or, if we may think collectively—of the Church's life. Here we achieve, venture, preach, sing, organize, administer. The other is related to the *passive* side of life. Here we submit, endure, suffer, wait. The history of Christian sanctity shows, I think, that not infrequently the critical test comes to us in this passive area of our experience. Here it is crucially revealed whether or not we are appropriating the full measure of strength offered us by our mighty Lord. Power to *do* and to *dare*? Wonderful! Power to *be* and to *bear*? Perhaps even more wonderful!

"Patience" and "longsuffering." Here is a choice morsel out of the rich Scottish past: "Patience," says James Spence of Aberdeen University, in his 1875 lectures on Colossians, "*patience* has its sphere of exercise especially in our relation to God, in the endurance of trial or in the waiting for promised blessing," while "*longsuffering* has its sphere of exercise especially in our relation to men, in the intercourse which binds us to each other."[1]

"Patience!" It is Job on the ash-pile, bereaved, blasted, and sore beset, yet nobly refusing to "curse God and die."

"Longsuffering!" It is Stephen in the pit of stoning, battered, defenceless, and dying, but using his failing breath to pray for his murderers, "Lord, lay not this sin to their charge!"

[1] James Spence, *Sunday Mornings With My Flock* (London: Hodder and Stoughton), pp. 36, 37.

Think, finally, of the *praise* with which Christ's power is to be accompanied. The final phrase of verse 11 and the first phrase of verse 12 are closely linked: "with joyfulness . . . giving thanks."

Endurance and longsuffering without any joy can be stern, stoical, and unappealing. St. Paul would have something finer in the testimony of these Colossian Christians. He would have their endurance touched with radiance, their suffering flavoured with praise.

In Calcutta I visited the Lee Memorial Orphanage. Many years ago, Mr. and Mrs. Lee went out from the States to India under the Methodist Board. Once, when they had taken a cottage in the foothills of the Himalayas to escape the heat of the plains, they left their six children for a few hours while they were away in the Master's service. A landslide occurred, the house was crushed, and the lives of all the children were taken. It was out of that devastating experience that these undefeated, unembittered, still thankful missionaries arose to say: "God has taken one family from us; He will give us another." Thus began the glorious work among Indian orphans that continues to this day. A dear friend of mine said that he once heard Mrs. Lee, addressing a large gathering of missionaries and national Christians, say, "I thank God for every sorrow that has come into my life!" My friend remarked, "There were tears in her eyes as she said it, but they were radiant tears!"

Ah, Paul, your prayer is still being answered—far beyond the borders of Colossae! You wanted the world to see in your fellow Christians a convincing consistency. You wanted them, therefore, to "walk worthy of the Lord unto all pleasing." That this might come to pass you wanted them to be filled and flooded with the knowledge of God's will. You wanted them thus to be fruitful in their testimony and fortified under testing. And in all of this you wanted them to experience the sweet and holy therapy of thankfulness, the cleansing wholesomeness of gratitude.

Is there any better way of influencing the Church toward

the highest than Paul's way of prayer? Do you know of any? Men may stiffen at threats and warnings. They may resist the logic of arguments. They may be cool to the eloquence of preaching. But must they not melt before long under the sunny fervour of the friend who prays for them out of passionate longing that their wills shall be attuned to God's will?

> *We know the paths wherein our feet should press,*
> *Across our hearts are written Thy decrees,*
> *Yet now, O Lord, be merciful to bless*
>   *With more than these.*
>
> *Grant us the will to fashion as we feel,*
> *Grant us the strength to labour as we know,*
> *Grant us the purpose, ribbed and edged with steel,*
>   *To strike the blow.*
>
> *Knowledge we ask not—knowledge Thou hast lent,*
> *But, Lord, the will—there lies our bitter need,*
> *Give us to build above the deep intent*
>   *The deed, the deed.*[1]

[1] John Drinkwater, from *Prayer Poems*, O. V. and Helen Armstrong, Abingdon-Cokesbury, 1942.

PRAYER AND THE WAY OF SANCTITY

"And the very God of peace sanctify you wholly; and I pray God your whole spirit and soul and body be preserved blameless unto the coming of our Lord Jesus Christ." 1 Thessalonians 5: 23.

IV

PRAYER AND THE WAY OF SANCTITY

PROFESSOR JOHN BAILLIE, in his *Invitation to Pilgrimage,* tells us that he finds himself "attempting to occupy a position somewhere between perfectionism on the one hand, and the renunciation of all sanctification on the other."

He then adds: "I am willing to confess that the reconnoitring of this intermediate position is the most delicate and difficult problem with which I am faced in my own personal life."

One has no quarrel with Dr. Baillie's candour and honesty. Those who know and love him would undoubtedly be the first to insist that they see in him those signs of Christlikeness that testify to an authentic Christian sanctity. Nevertheless, one cannot help confessing astonishment that any Christian, with his New Testament open before him, could ever seriously consider "the renunciation of all sanctification."

We must not forget that in the New Testament we have a whole portfolio of terms that speak to us of one aspect or another of the sanctification of God's children. The two most closely related are "holiness," or its cognate "holy," and "sanctification," or its cognates "sanctify" and "sanctified." In English terms, the one comes down to us from Old English and the other from Latin. Both are used to convey the meaning of their Hebrew and Greek originals, that meaning being "consecrated," "separated," or "purified."

But in addition to these New Testament terms there are others that designate some phase or another of Christian sanctification. One thinks of "perfect" and its noun "perfection," of "crucify," of "yield," of "present," of "filled" and "fulness," especially as related to the Holy Spirit's ministry in the Christian. These represent a whole range of teaching that is concerned with what God does with us *after* we gain entrance into the community of the redeemed and *before* we are translated to the community of the glorified.

Now all of the terms I have mentioned had a place in the vocabulary of St. Paul. So true is this, so *significantly* true indeed, that it would scarcely be exaggerating to say that the paramount burden of the Pauline epistles is the sanctification of the Church.

This burden found expression in his writings from the very beginning. If we had been following the historical order in which the Apostle carried on his correspondence, we should have begun with the prayer that is now before us. Here, in the very first of those matchless letters that were to flow from his pastorally ministrant heart, we have a prayer for the full sanctification of Christians that not one of us, be he theologian or ploughman, can afford to treat lightly. Listen to it in the Revised Standard Version:

"May the God of peace himself sanctify you wholly; and may your spirit and soul and body be kept sound and blameless at the coming of our Lord Jesus Christ."

Hear it in the Berkeley New Testament:

"And may the God of peace himself make you holy through and through. May your spirit be without a flaw and your soul and body be maintained blameless for the coming of our Lord Jesus Christ."

Hear it in Phillips:

"May the God of peace make you holy through and through. May you be kept in soul and mind and body in spotless integrity until the coming of our Lord Jesus Christ."

I

Consider the *historical context* of this prayer.

On this point there are three observations I want to make:

1. Plainly, this was an intercession *in behalf of Christians*. It is impossible to doubt this if one remembers the spiritual

"birth certificate" that St. Paul has written out for them in the first chapter of the epistle. His heart brimming with gratitude and his mind warm with memories that blessed and burned, the evangelist reviews the story of their conversion. He piles up the happy evidences of it till no proof is wanting. Having "turned" from their "idols," they are "in God the Father and in the Lord Jesus Christ." This is witnessed by their "work of faith, and labour of love, and patience of hope." In virtue of these demonstrated graces their influence and example have become a kind of holy by-word in all the province. And, although they get some stinging persecution, they find an anodyne for their pain in the "joy of the Holy Ghost."

This I know of you, writes Paul, and it fills me with jubilant song. I know it from what I saw with my own eyes when I was with you. I know it also from the report of you that Timothy has just brought back to me.

Now, should such a conversion experience be conserved and its full possibilities be drawn out? Should such converts be shepherded into the green pastures of God's best for them? If so, then a prayer for their complete and continuing sanctification is not out of order.

2. Our second observation must be made—and will be heard, I trust—with intense care: not only is this a prayer for Christians, it is a prayer *for Christians whose sanctification, in principle and in fact, must be recognized as having already begun.*

It is no graveyard secret that any serious discussion of the theme of "holiness" must take account of opposing views of doctrine and more or less contradictory interpretations of experience. Why is this? The learned scholar may ask it with curious detachment. The plain seeker after truth asks it often with a touch of bewilderment if not of disgust.

Well, is it not fair to say that one reason for our differences is that we tend—all of us in some degree, I suspect—to be more rigidly analytical and theological than the Scriptures themselves? It is difficult for us to be content with those living

tensions within which the Holy Word holds both phases of
a truth that we want to separate out into sharp differentiations.

For example, it is not uncommon in some victorious life
circles to say to a Christian, "You may be justified, but are
you sanctified?" I can assure you that St. Paul would never
ask the question in that form. For no one taught more clearly
than he did that *all* those who are "in Christ" and who know
Christ to be in them are sanctified.

To be sure, they are justified—forgiven and reckoned to be
righteous in view of the atonement made by God's well
beloved Son. But, just as truly, they are sanctified—separated
from an old life and made to belong to God through the
imparted life of the crucified and risen Lord. Paul's word to the
Corinthians must be taken seriously: "And such were some
of you ('thieves, covetous, drunkards,' etc.): but ye are washed,
but ye are sanctified, but ye are justified in the name of the
Lord Jesus, and by the Spirit of our God" (1 Corinthians 6: 11).
That the measure of their experimental sanctification left much
to be desired is clear enough from the complaints the Apostle
is obliged to lodge against them, but there it is nevertheless.

The principle of sanctification is *separation*—renouncing
what is known to be contrary to the life we have received from
God. The process of sanctification is that of *assimilation*—
growing likeness to the perfect image of our divine Lord.
Thus we say that in principle and in process, as well as in
position ("in Christ"), every Christian may be said to be sanctified. It is therefore not precisely for this that Paul is praying.

3. And now our third observation with respect to the
context of this prayer: it is a prayer *for Christians to whom
Paul has just proposed a pattern of sanctity that is high but not
too high.* What is this pattern? I want you to see it for yourself,
beginning with verse 13, and using the Phillips rendering:

"Live together in peace" (v. 13). Not all Christians do, but
they should. Bad attitudes in personal relationships—
jealousies that rankle and bitternesses that fester—are signs
that the full victoriousness of sanctification is somehow being
missed.

"Be very patient with all men" (v. 14). Why not? Ill temper in Christians is neither necessary nor nice. All the pious rationalizations in the world can never make it anything but ill-fitting for Christ's man.

Pastor Bernhard Helland, a ministerial friend of the Lutheran communion in Minneapolis, has served as a missionary in India. He tells of the night when, shortly after his arrival in that land, he sat until a late hour with a veteran missionary whose counsel was to prove immensely helpful. "One thing I want to tell you at the beginning of your work in the Orient," said this seasoned servant of God. "It is this: lose your temper and you lose all. These people of India may not always hold their tempers, but they expect us to keep ours." "Thirty years later," says Pastor Helland, "I asked a Santali doctor why this statement was so true. His reply was: 'Perhaps I cannot explain why it is true, but I can tell you that it is indeed true. My people look down upon a man, especially a man of leadership, who loses his temper. And more than that, we have a peculiar way of withdrawing from a man who gets angry. We feel in a way that he has insulted us, and so we just draw away from him.'" Pastor Helland then added: "Now I could understand what the Bible means when it says, 'Have nothing to do with a man of anger.'"

St. Paul's point is that ill-tempered Christians need not be ill-tempered. They have no business to be ill-tempered.

"Be sure that no one repays a bad turn by a bad turn" (v. 15). To return bad for bad is carnivorous—animal-like. To return good for good is cultural—calculating. To return good for bad is Christian—holy.

"Be happy in your faith at all times" (v. 16). A typically empty, bored American sophisticate of the female variety became a transformed person. Someone gave her the clue to the Spirit-filled life. Her radiance, even when an accident robbed her of her husband, was phenomenal. Writing about a spiritually needy friend, she said: "I do wish I could share all the joy in my heart with her. She deserves it, and I have enough for ten people!"

"Never stop praying" (v. 17). You don't stop breathing—not, at any rate, unless you are prepared to engage in the enormity of suicide. Prayer, as the fine hymn has it, is "the Christian's vital breath, the Christian's native air." That many of us are irregular and careless about our "prayers" is shabbily true. Roman Catholics are ecclesiastically required to practise the "holy habits," prayers and readings. Many Protestants, rightfully doubting the value of "mechanical" devotions, are disgracefully content to feed the soul by whim and caprice. Hence our rolls are crowded with the names of spiritual starvelings.

"Be thankful, whatever the circumstances may be" (v 18). Luther once said, "When I cannot pray, I sing." Thankfulness, contrary to what some of us imagine, is not the rhapsody of hilarious emotion, but the steady music of humility. It is the prevailing mood of anyone who has once for all waked up to the fact that he is in debt to somebody for everything. As a friend of mine says, "We are all in debt to the universe; we have nothing that we did not receive."

"Quench not the Spirit" (v. 19), or, better, "Never damp the fire of the Spirit," as Phillips has it. What the Apostle means by his admonition is made clear in what follows: "Never despise what is spoken in the name of the Lord. By all means use your judgment, and hold on to whatever is really good" (Phillips). From the days of the Apostle until now the question of *form* versus *spontaneity* has had to be faced. The Church has its free Pentecostals and it has its formal Anglo-Catholics. Shall we say, in a quick theft from Kipling, "And never the twain shall meet?" Not if we are Pauline! The spiritually *creative* and the spiritually *conventional* are not sworn enemies. They only war on each other when each goes to excess. Whatever we do, we must not put the Holy Ghost in a strait-jacket. Form without flame is Christianity turned cadaverous.

"Abstain from every form of evil" (v. 18). This reading of the Revised Standard Version is much to be preferred. When are we going to take the New Testament seriously in such

passages as this? When are we going to let it "sink in" that this is not a piece of moralistic idealism? This is an evangelical imperative! As Professor Newton Flew has it in his study of holiness in the writings of St. Paul, "It is not impossible (as he knows very well) for one to step down from the lofty level of life in the Spirit to the fetters and filth of the old life. But it is unnecessary."

Here, then, in these living lineaments, we see the pattern of Christian sanctity. If the level on which we see it is higher than that on which the *average* Christian lives, let it be speedily added that it is not higher than that on which the *normal* Christian may live. Here is the *norm!* When we live below it, we are sub-normal.

Professor James W. Clarke, of Princeton Theological Seminary, commenting on this very passage in Thessalonians, says something about this subnormality: "So many of us Christians are going through life at half or three-quarter pressure. We are thought to be alive, and are partly dead. We make religious affirmations, but are defective in religious conduct and service. We are, like Ananias, keeping back part of the price, for we are split in our enthusiasms, divided in our minds, and faltering in our loyalties ... We need reconsecration to God."

Professor Clarke calls it "reconsecration." I like better what St. Paul calls it, and to that we now turn.

II

We must examine what I shall call the *central concern* of this prayer. This concern embraces two tremendous realities: (1) a *holiness* which God decisively shares with His children and (2) a *wholeness* which He dynamically sustains in His children.

Consider the first: *a holiness that God decisively shares with those who are already positionally and processively sanctified.* Weymouth's rendering is vigorous and unafraid: "And may the God of peace himself make you entirely holy."

F

The one thing that is not brought out clearly, just because it is so difficult to do so, is the aorist tense of the Greek verb.

Many of you will have in your libraries, and will have read, Evan Hopkins' volume entitled *The Law of Liberty In The Spiritual Life,* which is so often regarded as a kind of compendium of Keswick teachings. In the Appendix there are some "Notes," among which you will find one on "the Greek aorist." A scholar is quoted who says, in part, "The aorist always denotes a point in contradistinction to a line."

"A point!"

Let the man who quotes the Greek scholar be also the man who testifies to the great hour. It was in the year 1873. It occurred in Curzon Chapel, London. Evan Hopkins, thirteen years along the way of discipleship since that day when a coastguardsman had introduced him to Christ and the new life in Christ, now hears a message on the subject of holiness. That night there was made to him a disclosure of the Lord Jesus so strong, convicting and compelling that the experience associated with it was like passing from the wilderness into the Promised Land.

That night, far into the night, he sat with Mrs. Hopkins, telling her of the mighty thing God had done in him. He told her that the text which the Holy Spirit had used to bring amazing release and fulfilment to his struggling, divided soul was 2 Corinthians 9: 8, "And God is able to make all grace abound toward you; that ye, always having all sufficiency in all things, may abound to every good work." The inclusive sweep of this promise evoked a matching faith from the heart of this servant of God and a new stage in his spiritual pilgrimage began.

As Mrs. Hopkins put it, "Christ had indeed become to him 'the Fountain within' springing up. It was not merely that his Lord would help him. It was that he would do *all,* and would live in him His holy life—the only holy life possible to us, as he would often say."[1]

[1] Alexander Smelie, *Evan Henry Hopkins—A Memoir* (Marshall Brothers Ltd., London), p. 54.

A point!

Reference has been made in a previous chapter to Dr. A. B. Simpson, whose flaming missionary statesmanship gave rise, under God, to the Christian and Missionary Alliance. His writings on the life of sanctification have notably enriched the whole body of the Church's literature on Christian sanctity. Let this Presbyterian minister give his witness:

"I shall never forget the morning that I spent in my church reading an old musty book I had discovered in my library on the subject *The Higher Christian Life*. I had struggled long and vainly with my own intense nature, my strong self-will, my peculiar temptations. My spiritual life had been a constant humiliation. I had talked to my people about the deeper things of the Spirit, but there was a hollow ring, and my heart was breaking to know the Lord Jesus as a living bright reality.

"As I pored over that little volume, I saw a new light. The Lord Jesus revealed Himself as a living and all-sufficient presence, and I learned for the first time that Christ had not saved us from future peril, and left us to fight the battle of life as best we could; but He who had justified us was waiting to sanctify us, to enter into our spirit, and substitute His strength, His holiness, His love, His joy, His faith, His power, for all our worthlessness, helplessness and nothingness, and make it an actual living fact. 'I live, yet not I, but Christ liveth in me.' It was indeed a new revelation.

"Throwing myself at the feet of the glorious Master, I claimed the mighty promise—'I will dwell in you and walk in you.' Across the threshold of my spirit there passed a Being as real as the Christ who came to John on Patmos, and from that moment a new secret has been the charm and glory and strength of my life and testimony . . . I have learned the secret, 'I can do all things through Christ which strengtheneth me.'"

Please hold back for a moment the questions raised by such testimonies as these. Before the queries or the quibbles, let's have the central verities. Here are men of the faith, men of

the new life, men "in Christ," and therefore sanctified, who
nevertheless experienced a crucial disclosure of the Divine
holiness. The sanctifying God *acted*. They became the con-
scious subjects of that action. God, in His Holy Spirit, was
let loose within them with a penetrating and purifying pos-
sessedness that marked off a decisively new stage in their
communion with Him.

If their experience was something you do not understand,
at least deny yourself the right to despise it. If you do not
long for it, at least do yourself the fairness of asking what
manner of Christian you are, after all. If you have experienced
something that corresponds to it, if the shining secret has
been unlocked to your up-yielding soul, then do the good
Davidic thing and call on all that is within you to "bless his
holy name," or, with Charles Wesley sing:

> *From all iniquity, from all,*
> *He shall my soul redeem;*
> *In Jesus I believe, and shall*
> *Believe myself to Him.*

But now, the central concern of St. Paul's prayer relates to
something more than the holiness which God decisively shares
with His children. It relates also to *a wholeness which God
dynamically sustains in His children.* Here are the relevant
words of the prayer: "and I pray God your whole spirit and
soul and body be preserved blameless unto the coming of our
Lord Jesus Christ."

The Greek word translated "whole" is emphatic. "In the
entirety of your being" the Apostle is saying in effect, "God
will work out His sanctifying purpose in you and thus ready
you for the coming again of His Son, the Lord Jesus!"

Writers without number have multiplied words without
limit in the attempt to tell us precisely what St. Paul means
by the distinctive terms "spirit" and "soul" and "body."
Especially formidable is the difficulty of drawing satisfactory
lines of separation between the "spirit" and the "soul." It is
beyond the scope of this study to examine the matter

thoroughly. I shall have to be content with an observation or two and a quotation.

We are right, I am persuaded, in insisting that in the final analysis there are two orders of reality: *matter* and *spirit*. From this point of view—the metaphysical, if you will have it so—man consists of a material and an immaterial component. He is a living fusion or synthesis of the spiritual and the material. God in creation has given him a composition of "dust" (the material) and "living soul" (the spiritual).

But the immaterial side of man's nature is sometimes viewed in Scripture as being, functionally, a dual thing. In the passage before us and in Hebrews 4: 12 we have the "spirit" distinguished from the "soul." It is at this point that a quotation from Dr. Griffith Thomas serves a useful purpose:

"The spirit is that inmost part of our life which is related to God. The soul is the inner life regarded in itself as the seat and sphere of intellect, heart and will."

Dr. Thomas adds: "The body is the outward vehicle and expression of the soul and spirit through which we are enabled to serve God."

I give you this statement not because I think it clears up all mysteries or because I think it is beyond all criticism, but because it puts simply—perhaps too simply—a truth that no scholar has found easy to clarify.

We are on clear Biblical ground, I believe, if we regard the spirit as that highest capacity in man by means of which he is constituted the carrier of God's image. The "fall," that is, the prideful estrangement of man from God, has defaced this image but has not destroyed it. The spirit, moreover, is preeminently the carrier of the "life" of God conceived in terms of communion and fellowship. The "fall," by breaking this communion, left the human spirit destitute of life, "dead in trespasses and sin." It is upon the spirit, therefore, that the Holy Ghost operates in the new birth, restoring the life of God and elevating the spirit once more to the level of control and ascendancy over the other powers—physical, emotional and volitional—of the redeemed man's being.

But I am in danger of leading you too far afield. The point of real urgency that now confronts us is this: in the life of entire sanctification there is an unfolding continuity and progression in which the Spirit of God dynamically sustains the *whole* man in a victorious fellowship with his Lord.

This victoriousness is not to be made the equivalent of perfectness or of faultlessness, much less of temptationlessness. Its carefully chosen qualification lies in the word "blameless," which has the force of an adverb. "I pray that your whole spirit and soul and body"—your God-vitalized, God-possessed personality—"be preserved blameless" in a moment-by-moment fellowship with Himself, "unto the coming of our Lord Jesus Christ."

You remember the lovely benediction of Jude: "Now unto him that is able to keep you from falling . . ." That corresponds to St. Paul's "preserve you blameless." It is for the *here* and *now*. It is today's faith overcoming the world. It is this hour's communion with the indwelling Christ by which temptation is met and mastered. It is this moment's cleansing by the blood of the Cross, answering for all our utter unworthiness and our acknowledged imperfectness.

But then Jude goes beyond all this: "Unto him that is able to keep you from falling, and to present you *faultless* before the presence of his glory with exceeding joy" (Jude 24).

Mark the distinction: preserved "blameless" *now*, presented "faultless" *then*. But let us not be over-enamoured of *words* —even those most carefully chosen. Our concern, finally, must be with Biblical realities and their relationship to actual living. After we have sifted out the faultlessness and disclaimed it for all of us mortals, does the blamelessness that remains in St. Paul's prayer describe what is *actual* in the lives of those who have said a vast "Yes" to the sanctifying God, or only what is *possible*?

Each of us must answer for himself. I am persuaded the possibility is there *for all of us*. Nor do I doubt that the sustained actuality is there for some of us, though not for many. Yet this should neither deter nor discourage the rest of us. This fulness of the sanctifying Spirit is, after all, a dynamic, not a static, experience. It is a relative, not an absolute. Its authentic force is ever dependent upon the live contact between the Christian and the Holy Spirit, answering to the contact between the trolley and the wire. The flowing of the current an hour ago means nothing *now* if the trolley is "off."

Hence the necessity of continuing adjustment to the unfolding will of God and the offered ministry of the Holy Spirit in the ongoing life of the Christian. Given this adjustment, the constancy of victory is something not to be denied.

The testimony of Evan Hopkins can help us again. The year of his deeper crisis was 1873. In 1913—just four decades later—he was at Keswick. He opened one of his addresses by saying:

"I think I ought to be the most thankful man in this tent, because I am privileged to testify that the blessing lasts. It has lasted with me forty years. I shall never forget that sacred spot where the first consecration meeting was held, in London in May, 1873. I had been converted thirteen years, brought to the Lord through a coastguardsman, and I had learned the need of my own heart during those years. At the time that I refer to I was immensely stirred to seek this blessing. We had heard about it, and there in Curzon Chapel, Mayfair, under the gallery, sixteen well-known Christian people met together. ... This was just the beginning of the movement, and I ought to be one of the most thankful men in this tent, because of God's gracious keeping power for forty years. I want to bear testimony to that fact, and give Him all the glory. There have been many failures. I am not glorying in self, but what was revealed to me that day—the all-sufficiency of Christ—is as precious to my soul as it ever was."[1]

III

Having looked at its historical context and having exposed ourselves to its central concern, we cannot take leave of this

[1] *The Keswick Week*, 1913, p. 122.

prayer for the Thessalonians without bracing ourselves with its *effectual confidence*: "faithful is he that calleth you, who also will do it."

There are at least three variant readings that I want you to take:

Hear Phillips: "May the God of peace make you holy through and through. May you be kept in soul and mind and body in spotless integrity until the coming of our Lord Jesus Christ. He who calls you is utterly faithful and He will finish what He has set out to do."

Consider Moffatt: "May the God of peace consecrate you through and through! Spirit, soul, and body, may you be kept without break or blame till the arrival of our Lord Jesus Christ! He who calls you is faithful, He will do this."

And then Conybeare: "Now may the God of peace Himself, sanctify you wholly; and may your spirit and soul and body be preserved blameless at the appearing of our Lord Jesus Christ. Faithful is He who calls you; He will fulfil my prayer."

Is there the least shadow of a doubt in our minds that God's calling is to holiness? With the New Testament open before us, uncertainty on this score would appear strange backwardness, if not strange blindness.

God calls us to the *position* of holiness: "But of him are ye in Christ Jesus, who of God is made unto us wisdom, righteousness, sanctification, and redemption" (1 Cor. 1: 30).

God calls us to the *practice* of holiness: "For this is the will of God, even your sanctification, that ye should abstain from fornication," or, as Phillips has it, "God's plan is to make you holy, and that entails first of all a clean cut with sexual immorality," following which, only a few sentences away, comes the even stronger word, "The calling of God is not to impurity but to the most thorough purity, and anyone who makes light of the matter is not making light of a man's ruling but of God's command" (1 Thess. 4: 3, 7, 8).

God calls us to the *partnership* of holiness: "But you are a chosen race, a royal priesthood, a holy nation, a people belonging to God, that you may make known the perfections of him who hath called you out of darkness into his marvellous light" (1 Peter 2 : 9).

God calls us to the *passion* of holiness: "God has given me that genuine righteousness which comes from faith in Christ. How changed are my ambitions! Now I long to know Christ and the power shown by His Resurrection: now I long to share His sufferings, even to die as He died, so that I may perhaps attain, as He did, the resurrection from the dead. Yet, my brothers, I do not consider myself to have 'arrived,' spiritually, nor do I consider myself already perfect. But I keep going on, grasping ever more firmly that purpose for which Christ grasped me. My brothers, I do not consider myself to have fully grasped it even now. But I do concentrate on this: I leave the past behind and with hands outstretched to whatever lies ahead I go straight for the goal— my reward the honour of being called by God in Christ" (Philippians 3 : 9–14, Phillips).

And God calls us, as we have seen at the very heart of this prayer, to the *penetration* of holiness: "the God of peace Himself make you entirely holy" (Weymouth).

What remains? Just one thing: our confidence to meet His calling—and His doing!

I come to this closing moment with a light heart and yet— so strange are the paradoxes of life—with a heavy heart. It is a heart of concern.

The concern is that the mystery of our unanswered questions shall not keep us from the reality of that holy release which some of us so desperately need this moment. It is concern that our disagreements shall not bristle with a controversial sharpness, and so cause us to miss the blessing.

If I tell you that there is a deep crucifying of your troublesome and unsubdued ego that you may have here and now by renouncing struggle and taking the victory of Christ by faith, is there not danger of "quietism"—of just imagining that the sanctified life is a kind of glorified picnic in which I am passive recipient and God is active giver? There is. To guard against this excess, I must know that the full release from the bondage of self which I now claim by faith will neither complete my redeemed character nor put an end to the necessity of constant watchfulness and discipline.

If I tell you that being cleansed from all sin is a faith-gift from your Heavenly Father which you may have at this moment, does it mean that your future is one of sinlessness? Is this "eradication," "sinless perfection"? For most of us the terms are emotionally "loaded" and carry a somewhat varying theological twist. I make no issue of any term not taken from the Biblical text. "Eradication" has overtones I do not like. "Sinless perfection" has dimensions and stringency that make it becoming for One only—our blessed Lord.

Yet it is possible for us to suffer from excess of caution, fear, and downright unbelief. If there is subtle peril in too much preoccupation with one's own holiness (and there is!), is there not, also, a strange danger in too much preoccupation with our confessed sinfulness? One of our neo-orthodox scholars, insisting that God can do nothing with sin but perpetually to forgive it, says that with his dying breath he hopes to say, "God, be merciful to me a sinner." On hearing this, a friend of mine, who knows both the pitfalls of the sanctified and the power of the Sanctifier, remarked gently, "I cannot agree. It is my hope that my dying word will be, 'My Lord, and my God!'"

In the collective Christian mind that comes to light in the epistles one does not find a sin-fixation but a Christ-fixation. Not the incurable persistence of carnality but the illimitable triumph of Calvary! Not *sin* reigns but *grace* reigns!

"Faithful is he that calleth you, who also will do it!" There it stands! And St. Teresa, I doubt not, would have made St. Paul happy with her ringing proclamation: "We can never have too much confidence in our God: as we hope in Him so shall we receive."

PRAYER AND THE WAY OF EXPECTANCY

"Wherefore also we pray always for you, that our God would count you worthy of this calling, and fulfil all the good pleasure of his goodness, and the work of faith with power: That the name of our Lord Jesus Christ may be glorified in you, and ye in him, according to the grace of our God and the Lord Jesus Christ."

2 Thessalonians 1 : 11–12.

PRAYER AND THE WAY OF EXPECTANCY

V

WHEN all of the prayers of St. Paul are taken together, it becomes clear that they are as astonishing
in their sweep and range as they are in their depth
and power. It would be hard to think of a phase of the
Christian's life or of the Church's experience that is left
unnoticed.

In the supplication before us a curtain is drawn aside and
we are given a view of what theologians sometimes call "last
things." Is God working out a purpose? Has history a goal?
Will the Kingdom of God be unveiled in triumphant consummation? Is there, with respect to the future, an *expec-
tancy* of faith that has in it any more substance or behind it
any more warrant than the credulous yearnings of our wistful
spirits?

To all of these queries the Apostle Paul answers with a
resounding "Yes." Such is the effect, I take it, of these words
of the prayer, which I give you in the Berkeley Version: "We
constantly pray for you, that our God may render you worthy
of His call, and by His power may fulfil every desire for
goodness and every faith-inspired effort" (v. 11). In the word
"fulfil" you have the pith and point of the matter. God's
last word will not be either failure or futility; it will be
fulfilment.

We shall see in a moment that these Thessalonians were
passing through the fire. Their faith was being severely
tested. Life for them was under siege from Satan. In these
circumstances the prayer of their great friend and spiritual
counsellor is that they may not lose heart, that, instead, they
may be unshaken in the confidence that God is working

through them to bring His holy purpose to a victorious conclusion.

His love in times past forbids me to think
He'll leave me at last in trouble to sink;
While each Ebenezer I have in review
Confirms His good pleasure to help me quite through.

This may not be great poetry—many of our fine hymns are *not*—but it does state rather exactly what it is that was in St. Paul's view as he prayed.

I

Let us set our minds, first of all, on the *reasons* that underlie this prayer.

There's a logic about it that we ought not to miss, for the Apostle begins, according to the Authorized Version, with the word "Wherefore." "To this end," says the RSV, while Weymouth gives the rendering, "It is with this in view."

Why should there be a prayer for these Christians that God would "count" them "worthy of this calling, and fulfil all the good pleasure of his goodness, and the work of faith with power"?

The double reason for it was that there was something *gloomy* through which they were passing and something *glorious* towards which they were nevertheless moving.

1. *A present burdened with difficulty.* Dwell on that for a moment. It helps to explain the apostolic concern for these comrades at Thessalonica. In verse 4 notice is taken of the "persecutions and tribulations" that they are enduring. In verse 5 it is acknowledged that they are being made to "suffer" for the kingdom of God, while· in verse 7 it is recognized that they are "troubled."

Let us set this down in indelible ink: in the Christian life *comfort* and *challenge, trust* and *trouble,* are never far apart.

Our Lord made this clear. "In the Sermon on the Mount,"

wrote Dr. W. R. Maltby, "Jesus promised his disciples three
things—that they would be entirely fearless, absurdly happy,
and that they would get into trouble. They did get into
trouble, and found, to their surprise, that they were not
afraid."

St. Paul was no less clear in his "briefing" of his converts
on the tasks and perils of the life in Christ. Part of his
ministry, he assures us, consisted in "Confirming the souls of
the disciples, and exhorting them to continue in the faith,
and that we must through much tribulation enter into the
kingdom of God" (Acts 14: 22).

No faith is mature if it thinks only of answers to prayer
that come in the form of *escape* from loss and sorrow and
pain. A London minister tells of a father whose son was
fighting with the forces in France. "At our prayer meetings,"
said the pastor, "he would earnestly pray that God would
hide that soldier son beneath His wings. He once added with
deep tenderness, 'The bullet was never made that can pierce
Thy wings.' But the boy was killed all the same."

If this shakes us and threatens to turn confidence into
cynicism, we should review the Bible's *magnum opus* on faith,
the eleventh chapter of Hebrews. True, it tells of those who
"through faith escaped the edge of the sword, out of weakness were made strong, waxed valiant in fight, turned to flight
the armies of the aliens" (v. 34). But have you noticed the
significance of a little phrase of two words that occurs twice—
"and others"? "And others were tortured, not accepting
deliverance. And others had trials of cruel mockings and
scourgings, yea, moreover, of bonds and imprisonment; they
were stoned, they were sawn asunder, were tempted, were
slain with the sword" (vv. 35–37).

No wonder George Tyrell once set it down boldly: "To
believe that this terrible machine world is really from God,
in God, and unto God, and that through it and in spite of
its blind fatality all works for good—that is faith in long
trousers."

It is because I know your faith has got to grow up, cries

St. Paul, in effect, that I am praying for you. The faith that
escapes trouble is often honoured of God, but, equally, the
faith that *endures* trouble.

2. *A prospect bright with delight.* In verses 7 and 10 the
eyes of these persecuted Christians are lifted from present
gloom to future glory : "to you who are troubled rest with us,
when the Lord Jesus shall be revealed from heaven with his
mighty angels . . . when he shall come to be glorified in his
saints, and to be admired in all of them that believe (because
our testimony among you was believed) in that day."

The doctrine of the return and ultimate reign of Christ
had been misunderstood by many of these Thessalonian
Christians. The errors in their thinking and the excesses in
their conduct had to be corrected by the Apostle. They must
learn not to interpret the immediacy of the return in such
fashion as to unfit them for the ordinary responsibilities and
activities of life. Bread and butter must be earned. Rooms
must be tidied up. Children must be reared. The world must
learn the good news of Christ's *first* coming.

Nevertheless, the prospect of His return must never be
despised or dimmed. For it holds God's answer to many a
mystery. The second advent, on its judgment side, will bring
inevitable retribution on the workers of iniquity, however
immune to punishment they may appear to have been. And,
on its *rapture* side, it will bring vindication, honour, and
glory to the children of God, however unjustly and cruelly
they may have been treated by the world.

Hear Paul's putting of the matter, as rendered by Phillips :
"His justice will one day repay trouble to those who have
troubled you, and peace to all of us who, like you, have
suffered. This judgment will issue eventually in the terrific
denouement of Christ's personal coming from Heaven with
the angels of His power. It will bring full justice in dazzling
flame upon those who have refused to know God or to obey
the Gospel of our Lord Jesus Christ. . . . But to those whom
He has made holy His coming will mean splendour unimaginable (vv. 6-8, 10).

Here, then, is our prospect, all luminous and luring: "His coming will mean splendour unimaginable."

But what, it may be asked, is the connection between the difficult present and the delightful future; and what is the link between both of these considerations and the prayer that the Apostle is offering?

The clue is located, it seems to me, in the fifth verse, which Phillips renders thus: "Without doubt He intends to use your suffering to make you worthy of His Kingdom." Let comment on the particular meaning of the word "worthy" be reserved until it comes up under another heading. Meanwhile, the core of St. Paul's concern is that these Christians may really see that their capacity for making a creative and victorious use of suffering here is related to their capacity to share in the meaningful glory of Christ's return and reign afterwhile. My intercession for you, says Paul, is to the end that you may grasp the Divine intention: God "intends to use your suffering to make you worthy of His Kingdom." It is *that* which saves pain from sheer senselessness and persecution from naked cruelty.

II

If these be the reasons for St. Paul's concern, what now are the specific *requests* that form the substance of this supplication?

They are two in number:

1. There is the prayer for the *Divine favour*: "that our God would count you worthy of this calling."

The phrase "this calling" becomes "his call" in some versions and "your calling" in others. The difference is not as important as the underlying fact, which is that God, through the Gospel of His Son, has summoned us to reconciliation with Himself and to an eventual reigning with Him in a finalized phase of His Kingdom.

Repentance is in this call: "I am not come to call the righteous, but sinners to repentance" (Matt. 9: 13).

The Cross as saving power is in this call: "We preach Christ

G

crucified, unto the Jews a stumbling-block, and unto the Greeks foolishness; but unto them which are called, both Jews and Greeks, Christ the power of God and the wisdom of God" (1 Cor. 1 : 23, 24).

Freedom from legalistic and ceremonial bondage is in this call: "For, brethren, ye have been called unto liberty" (Gal. 5: 13).

Practical holiness is in this call: "For God hath not called us unto uncleanness, but unto holiness" (1 Thess. 4: 7).

Peaceableness in Christian relationships is in this call: "And let the peace of God rule in your hearts, to the which also ye are called in one body" (Col. 3: 15).

And, finally, *sharing in His eternal kingdom and glory* is in this call: "God . . . hath called you unto his kingdom and glory" (1 Thess. 2: 12).

Now "this calling," to use the word of the Authorised Version, is sometimes brought forward in Scripture as something that has taken place in the past and sometimes as a thing that is taking place in the present. When, for example, in the chapter that follows our prayer the Apostle says, "God hath from the beginning chosen you to salvation through sanctification of the Spirit and belief of the truth, whereunto he called you by our Gospel," both verbs—"chosen" and "called"—are in the past tense.

On the other hand, in the clause already quoted from 1 Thessalonians 2: 12, although the Authorized Version renders it "called," the verb is actually in the present tense. Hence in the Williams translation, where much stress is laid on accuracies and niceties of tense, the reading is "God who *calls* you into His Kingdom and His glory." This gives rise to a discerning observation in Ellicott's commentary: "The call is not simply a momentary act, but a *continual* beckoning upwards, until the privileges offered are actually attained." Or, as James Clarke puts it, "It (the Christian calling) is an eternal act, begins when a man knows he is face to face with God, effects a definite change in his character, and is a continuing and expanding experience."

God *has* called us, *is* calling us, *will* call us!

Consider now, in the light of all this, the meaning of the words "count you worthy." Two suggestions emerge. The first is that at every stage of the redeemed life we are the subjects of God's unmerited mercy, apart from which we should be doomed. It is not simply and solely at the beginning that we are "justified," or accounted righteous, for Christ's sake: it is all the way along! Theologians may speak learnedly about the difference between "imputed" and "imparted" righteousness, but the plain, practical, Biblical fact is that even what is "imparted"—the holiness of *desire* and *motive* and *character* woven into our lives by the Holy Spirit —is of God's undeserved grace. It is His doing!

Pope's words are to the point: "No change of character, no degree of holiness, even though reaching to an entire destruction of sin, avails to modify this essential relation. The saint is always and only reckoned to be holy: not because his holiness is other than real, but because the fact remains that he is and must ever be, with all his sanctity, only a sinner saved by grace."[1]

A friend of mine put it in much less formal terms when he said, "When I enter heaven at the last, I am going in on God's bankruptcy law—I didn't have what it takes, but He did!"

Consider the other suggestion that springs from the phrase "count you worthy," which is used seven times in the New Testament and twice in this opening chapter of the second Thessalonian letter. Some translations give us the reading "*make* you worthy." It is less accurate but it nevertheless speaks of something that almost certainly was in Paul's mind. Try altering the phrase so that it reads "make you fit." Rightly understood, this takes nothing away from the thought of *grace* as we just touched upon it.

At the same time it brings out a facet of truth that the New Testament proclaims over and over: whom God forgives He fashions, whom He delivers from hell He disciplines for heaven. "Thou hast a few names in Sardis, which have not

[1] Pope, *The Prayers of St. Paul*, (Chas. H. Kelly, London, 1896), p. 137.

defiled their garments; and they shall walk with me in white; for they are worthy" (Rev. 3: 4). On this it has been wisely remarked: "The word here rendered worthy does not mean merit but fitness."

Into this garment of fitness God weaves by strange threads the beauties and the strengths He desires. "If we suffer with him, we shall also reign with him:" *pain* is one of His threads. "If any man serve me, him will my Father honour:" *service* is a strand in the finished robe.

Somewhere I have read of a gentleman who began a study of butterflies. The cocoons of an extraordinarily beautiful specimen he placed where the spring sun would shine on them. Under the warmth the curious shells began to swell. One, a little in advance of the others, broke open and a butterfly appeared. Since this variety of butterfly was famed for the splendour of its colours, he was perplexed by the fact that the little creature's wings were drab. As it struggled to work itself free of the shell, he observed that it was being held by a tiny white cord. His penknife cut the thread and liberated the fragile struggler. It flew about the room; but as for glory of colour, there was none.

With the second cocoon he decided to let nature take its course. There was the same initial struggle, the same slender thread, the same seeming frustration on the part of the new-born insect. For more than an hour, said the gentleman, the little creature fought for its freedom. Even before the struggle was over, the colour began shooting out into its wings; and when at last the battle was won, those wings were simply glorious.

That story, it seems to me, casts a helpful light on what St. Paul is saying to these Thessalonians. I know "your patience and faith," he assures them, "in all your persecutions and tribulations that ye endure" (v. 4). But I know also *why* God is permitting these difficult and sometimes dismaying trials to come to you. It is that "ye may be counted worthy of the kingdom of God." And as for the time when He will adjudge you fit for your place of reward and of assignment to those higher services that belong to the "life everlasting," it will be when Christ shall "come to be glorified in his saints and to be admired in all them that believe" (v. 10).

It is this divine approval for which the Apostle is praying as he thinks ahead to the day of Christ's unveiling. As we think ahead to that day, let's try to remember: butterflies that mature without *battle* mature without *beauty*. Perhaps we should rather say: they don't mature!

2. This leads us to examine the second request that the Apostle includes in his intercession. It is the asking for the *Divine fulfilment:* "and fulfil all the good pleasure of his goodness, and the work of faith with power."

Here is a double clause on which the shadings of the modern translations provide a feast for the mind's inquiring eye:

Weymouth has it, "and by His power accomplish every desire for goodness and every work of faith."

Williams: "And by His power fully satisfy your every desire for goodness and complete every activity of your faith."

Berkeley: "and by His power may fulfil every desire for goodness and every faith-inspired effort."

Phillips: "that He will effect in you all that His goodness desires to do, and that your faith makes possible."

Phillips takes the doubtful liberty of making "goodness" the *source* of the desire instead of the *thing desired*. Both for simplicity and accuracy the rendering of the English Revised is preferable: "And fulfil every desire of goodness and every work of faith with power."

Here are the two hemispheres of a *whole* Christian life: the inner ("every desire of goodness") and the outer ("every work of faith"); the *aspiration* and the *attainment*.

It is the plight of too many Christians to dwell in the mean cell of small contentments. Languishing aspirations lead to no lofty attainments.

Excuses for it? Certainly! Christians who pursue holiness are either queer or are on the way to becoming so. As for those who profess it, they are either frauds or fools. And besides, saintly souls must spend hours in prayer; whereas I, as an ordinary person in a workaday world, do not have the time for these holy vigils. So we feel, and so we argue—to our unutterable loss.

The heights of Christlikeness elude us, not because they are so elusive, but because we are so accustomed to calling them so. Even big names in theology can be cited to encourage the view that God's work in *counting* us righteous (justification) is the gospel indeed but God's work in *making* us holy (sanctification) is a minor consideration which, the more we emphasize it, tends to make us Pharisees or crackpots. So the low aim wins the day. In vast sections of Protestantism Christian sanctification has been put away in the "deep freeze" of theological unconcern and practical indifference.

Whatever hour the clock has struck, it is high time that those who call themselves Christ's should pay less heed to the voices of ecclesiastical caution and worldly prudence, and far more heed to the witness and summons of the New Testament. It would in fact be the beginning of a new day in the Church if only we would follow the uncurbed, unchecked, unintimidated instincts of the soul that is "newborn" in Christ.

> *He wills that I should holy be;*
> *That holiness I long to feel,*
> *That full divine conformity*
> *To all my Saviour's righteous will.*

Let's remember that even the desire for holiness is the sign of holiness, for it is the mark of God upon us. The very desire is, in some sense, the beating of God's heart within us.

But, mind you, we do not reach the full meaning of this part of St. Paul's prayer if we think only of aspiration. There is *accomplishment* also. God will do more than grant "every desire of goodness:" He will "fulfil . . . every work of faith."

The scientific age into which we moved less than a century ago has been a boon to the *mechanics* of life but it has not been, equally, a boon to life's real *dynamics*. But a change is under way. Science is more humble. Its limitations are now more readily granted. There is less disposition to laugh out of court the invisibles and the imponderables. Faith, though never actually done away, may lift up her head with new boldness.

This is true, for example, in the field of *medicine* and *health*. "Faith healing" may still be thought of as something cornered by evangelists who pitch colossal tents and give out cards to assure you a place in the "healing line." If, however, that is all you know about "faith healing," you are simply not in step with the times. It is getting serious attention, in a variety of forms, from psychiatrists, physicians, theologians, and pastors. There are Episcopalian and Presbyterian churches in which no surprise is registered if the pastor announces a service of "prayer for the sick."

Or take it in our *international relations*. Is there not a new recognition, before the threat of atomic annihilation, that our civilization must be saved, if it is saved at all, by *faith*? That is to say, the spiritual resources that God has offered men all along—forgiveness, righteousness, compassion, humility, good-will—must be laid hold of, else we shall tumble to our doom in the abyss of atomic night.

We may not take this way of faith. Forces demonic and egoistic are against it. But at least we have no sound reason for setting limits on what could be done to lessen international tensions and preserve the peace if we were to take it.

Similarly, we need to listen to those voices of faith which encourage the confidence that God stands ready to end the *spiritual mediocrity* and *ineffectualness* of the Christian Church today. The personal and collective commitment that gives wholeness, integration, directedness to our lives *can* be made. The subduing and crucifying of our hurtful egoism *can* be experienced. The loving of God and our neighbour with "all" the "heart" *can* be realized. The private as well as the public disciplines that make for spiritual growth *can* be practised.

Let faith rout fear. Let faith claim her own—in Christ. Let faith prove that the promises of God are "Yea and Amen."

Dr. John L. Peters, in one of the latest books dealing with the much-misunderstood theme of "Christian perfection," has a concluding word that is timely and trenchant: "If it is presumptuous to profess the attainment of perfect love as one's own achievement, it is no less presumptuous to deny that the grace of God can bring the surrendered soul into perfect integration. Who can say what the grace of God can do? Who dares say what it cannot do? . . . Any attempt to impose arbitrary limits approaches impiety."[1]

One might well put at the head of those sentences St. Paul's glowing announcement: "Where sin abounded, grace did much more abound" (Rom. 5: 20). Or, with equal appropriateness, he might use the Apostle's prayer that now engages us: "And fulfil every desire of goodness and every work of faith with power."

> *Inspire the living faith,*
> *Which whosoe'er receives,*
> *The witness in himself he hath,*
> *And consciously believes;*
> *The faith that conquers all,*
> *And doth the mountain move,*
> *And saves whoe'er on Jesus call,*
> *And perfects them in love.*

III

Come now to examine the *results* that are to follow this prayer.

Two consequences take shape before the mind of the praying Apostle:

1. *God will be glorified in His people:* "That the name of our Lord Jesus Christ may be glorified in you." The context

[1]Peters, *Christian Perfection and American Methodism* (Abingdon, Nashville), p. 200.

requires us to say that this glorification of the Name has reference to the *future* when, as verse 10 puts it, Christ shall "come to be glorified in his saints." Then, in some climactic way, the whole redeemed Church will bear witness to the splendour of His Name who "loved us and gave Himself for us."

But what of the *present*? The question is not to be erased: are we Christians now adding any lustre to the Saviour's name? If the name stands for the nature and character and influence of Christ—and undoubtedly it does—what are we contributing to the reputation of our Lord?

When Dwight L. Moody invited Henry Drummond to speak at the Northfield Bible Conference, someone asked him, apprehensively, if he realized that Mr. Drummond held some views that differed from those taught at Northfield. Moody replied, "I cannot say that I agree with all his notions, but he is more like Jesus Christ than any man I know, and that is the reason why I want him at Northfield." St. Paul's prayer, as it appears in Phillips, was being answered: "That the Name of our Lord Jesus Christ may become more glorious through you."

Or take the testimony of a man who, in an earlier day, went to Clairvaux for a visit with the saintly Bernard. "I tarried a few days with him," said the gentleman, "and whichever way I turned my eyes I marvelled, and thought I saw a new heaven and a new earth. As soon as you entered Clairvaux you could feel that God was in the place."

Yes, there is a present, as there will be a future, glorifying of the matchless Name. And it doesn't come by seeking to *glorify* Him; it comes by seeking *Him*. The glory breaks through—you can't conceal it!—when He fills the vision and ravishes the soul.

2. The other result that the Apostle's intercession contemplates is this: *God's people will be glorified in His Son:* "and ye (glorified) in him."

The glory is reciprocal. Since Christ and His Church are mysteriously one, it is not surprising to learn that each adds to the honour and satisfaction of the other. His redeemed people are His glory and He is theirs.

Again, St. Paul's thought bears toward the future and the consummation of history in the revelation of the returning Lord. "He has set before you the prospect of sharing the glory of our Lord, Jesus Christ" (2 : 14, Phillips).

A prominent and priceless part of this "sharing" will be the unveiling of the Christian's new body. Philippians 3 : 20, 21 becomes, under the Phillips touch, a freshly moving passage: "our outlook goes beyond this world to the hopeful expectation of the Lord Jesus Christ. He will re-make these wretched bodies of ours to resemble His own glorious Body, by that power of His which makes Him the Master of everything that is."

They have never caught the full meaning of Christ's resurrection who think only of "immortality" and the "future life." There is nothing distinctively Christian about the belief in life after death. More than one pagan philosopher has stoutly defended it. What is unique in the Christian faith is the communication of the glory of our Lord's resurrected and resplendent body to the people whom He has redeemed, so that they too shall have bodies "fashioned like unto his own glorious body."

The powers, immunities, and activities of this "body of glory" are beyond our present knowledge. They are but hinted at in Scripture. Just the hints are hauntingly attractive. "It doth not yet appear what we shall be; but we know that, when he shall appear, we shall be like him; for we shall see him as he is" (1 John 3 : 2).

> *I dreamed that I was growing old*
> *   (It may be it was not a dream),*
> *I shivered in the frosty cold*
> *   And trembled in the summer beam;*
> *It cost me many a bitter sigh,*
> *Until I knew it was not I.*

The house my Maker for me made
  Received His likeness in its form;
His wisdom all its parts displayed,
  His beauty clothed its chambers warm;
It is not so fair as years go by:
What matter—for it is not I.

The lamps that light its rooms burn low,
  Its music sounds more dull of late,
And one—it may be friend or foe,
  Knocks loudly often at its gate;
I tremble then—I scarce know why,
My house he claims, it is not I.

I am indeed a dweller there,
  A winter and a summer guest;
Its rust and its decay I share,
  But cannot look therein to rest.
I'm sure to leave it by and by—
'Tis but my house—it is not I.

I sometimes think, when lying down,
  For the last time I lock the door,
And leave the home so long my own,
  That I shall find it yet once more
So changed and fair I scarce shall know
The home I lived in Long Ago.

This, not in whole but in part, is what it will mean for God's redeemed people to be glorified in His Son.

IV

Finally, there stands the tender yet towering *resource* to which the Apostle's prayer looks for its answer: "according to the *grace* of our God and the Lord Jesus Christ."

Grace is *derived* from God, but it is *disclosed* in Jesus Christ our Lord.

The closer we come to an understanding of our dependence upon God the more ready we are to confess that everything that really matters starts from God's side. That is what makes it grace. Even *faith*, which in a sense is *our* responsibility and act, is seen by St. Paul as being "not of ourselves" but "the gift of God." The Apostle can say this because he recognizes, as we should, the object of all saving faith—Jesus Christ—has been given to us by God, and that our act of believing is called forth by His act of revealing Himself as worthy of our trust.

As Baron von Hugel has put it, "the passion and hunger *for* God comes *from* God, and God answers it with Christ." This St. Paul believed and believed passionately. Hence he knew that if the great expectations to which his prayer for the Thessalonians gave expression were to be realized, it would be by the working of God's mercifully communicated power.

Are they to be counted "worthy" of God's "calling" in that day when the returning Christ is revealed? It will be by His grace.

Is there to be a fulfilment of "every desire for goodness"? It will be by His grace.

Is there to be a bringing to pass of "every work of faith," and that with "power"? It will be by His grace.

Is the "name of our Lord Jesus Christ" to be "glorified" in His redeemed people and are they to be "glorified" in Him? It will be by His grace.

For in that grace is infinitely more than a benevolent attitude on God's part. In that grace is mighty action: a Son given, a Cross raised, a Tomb emptied, a Comforter—even the Holy Spirit Himself—bestowed.

So that, at the last, when the final steps of the pilgrimage are being taken, no Christian soul can do other than cry, "Not unto us, O Lord, not unto us, but unto Thy name give glory!"

When Bishop Francis Asbury, the dauntless dean of the circuit-riders, the father of American Methodism, was near the end of his notably fruitful life, he said:

"Were I disposed to boast, my boastings would be found true. I was converted at the age of sixteen. At the age of eighteen I began to preach, and travelled some in Europe. At twenty-six I left my native land, bade adieu to my weeping parents, and crossed a boisterous ocean to spend the rest of my days in a strange land, partly settled by savages. In thirty years I have crossed the Allegheny Mountains fifty-eight times. I have slept in the woods and been without food and covering. Through the Southern states I have waded swamps and led my horse for miles, and in these journeys took cold that brought on the diseases that now prey on my body and must soon terminate in death. But my mind is still the same, that through the merits of Christ and by the grace of God I am saved."[1]

A little later, when he crossed the river beyond which lay the "Celestial City," it was with him as it was with "Mr. Honest," who, wading into the dark stream, called back to his friends with the triumphant shout: "Grace reigns!"

[1]Quoted by Turner, *The Gospel of the Grace of God*, (Broadman, Nashville), p. 38.

PRAYER AND THE WAY OF SERENITY

"And the Lord direct your hearts into the love of God, and into the patient waiting for Christ."

2 Thessalonians 3: 5.

"Now the Lord of peace himself give you peace always by all means. The Lord be with you all."

2 Thessalonians 3: 16.

VI

PRAYER AND THE WAY OF SERENITY

IN the United States the non-fiction books of recent publication that rate, on the whole, highest in popularity are those which bear such titles as *How To Stop Worrying and Start Living, Peace of Soul, The Way to Power and Poise, Peace of Mind, Beyond Anxiety, Understanding Fear,* and *A Guide To Confident Living.*

Does the demand for such books reflect the *abundance* of our peace or the *scarcity* of it? The latest in drugs is a whole spate of concoctions called "tranquilisers." Although they are not to be confused with sedatives, there is something suggestive of the times in the popular name that has been given to them. Read the turmoil of a nation's soul in the titles of its books and the labels on its drugs!

The life and culture of the first century, to which St. Paul addressed his Gospel, had neither the books nor the drugs, but they did have the anxiety and fretfulness from which both of these devices are presumed to offer some release or respite. Even the Christian community had its members who, alas, had not learned Christ's secret of the undistracted heart —the heart that is inwardly "at leisure from itself."

Hence the propriety and the healing grace of the two brief prayers with which the Apostle brings to a close his second letter to the Thessalonians. The two intercessions, though separated by nearly a dozen verses, may be thought of as closely linked. Both are concerned with the stability and tranquillity that St. Paul himself had found in his union with Jesus Christ. Both are offered within a context of disturbance and restlessness. And both are related to a remarkable supplication that comes at the close of the preceding chapter: "And may our Lord Jesus Christ Himself, and God our Father who

has loved us and has given us in His grace eternal consolation
and good hope, comfort your hearts and make you steadfast
in every good work and word" (2: 16, 17, Weymouth).

Once more, as we have seen again and again in the Pauline
prayers, the pastoral yearning comes tenderly, throbbing to
the fore: "You are my children, not less than my comrades,
in Christ. I know you are set in the midst of confusions and
stresses. But I know also that in the Christ you have trusted—
in His encompassing love and His enduring patience—there
are depths of serenity within which the inmost soul of you
can be bedded down and find its needed quiet. So my prayer
for you is this: 'May the Lord guide your hearts into the
love of God and into the patience of Christ. . . . And may
the Lord of peace Himself continually grant you peace in
every way' " (Weymouth).

Consider now what sort of peace this is, for which the
Apostle prays.

I

For one thing, it is peace *in the midst of distraction*. In this
noisy—and often noisome—world how futile is the wish for a
peace that is *externally* conditioned or guaranteed! With
respect to his surroundings the Christian's serenity is a
serenity, not *because of*, but *in spite of*!

Of this we have ample evidence in the situation of which
the Apostle is obliged to take notice as he writes to the
Thessalonians.

Take what we may call the *distraction of indecency*. St. Paul
felt its power. He knew that the Christians in Thessalonica
were feeling it. Hence he writes: "Brethren, pray for us, that
the word of the Lord may have free course and be glorified,
even as it is with you; and that we may be delivered from
unreasonable and wicked men" (3: 1, 2). Ellicott's *Commentary* translates it "these monstrous and depraved people."

The reference, clearly, is to the enraged and vengeful Jewish
"monsters" who are described by Luke in Acts 17: 5–9. "But
the Jews which believed not," says Luke, "moved with envy,

took unto them certain lewd fellows of the baser sort, and gathered a company, and set all the city in an uproar" (v. 5).

Peace in the midst of *that*! Can anyone have it? we are prone to ask. St. Paul's answer is, Yes! When he prays for it, he is not baying at the moon. He is confidently asking for the possible.

John Wesley, it is recorded, was one day preaching in an evil section of London, where raucous and ribald sensualities were in command, when two ruffians appeared at the edge of the crowd. "Who is this preacher?" they asked, roughly. "What right has he to come here spoiling our fun? . . . We'll show him." A moment or two later, each with a stone in hand, they began elbowing their belligerent way through the throng. But just when they were ready to "let fly" at Wesley's face, he began talking about the power of Christ to change the lives of sinful men. It is reported that, even as he was speaking, a "serene beauty spread over his face." The two men, obviously quite overcome by it, stood there momentarily, their arms poised in mid-air. Then one turned to the other, and said, "He ain't a man, Bill; he ain't a man." Their arms came down. The stones dropped from their hands. As Wesley continued to preach, the altered expression on their countenances spoke of the softness that had stolen into their hearts.

The sermon over, Mr. Wesley began making his way through the crowd. The path that the people respectfully opened for him brought him within arm's length of where these "teddy boys" of that day were standing. One of them, almost tenderly, reached out and touched the evangelist's coat. At that, Mr. Wesley paused, placed his hands on the heads of the lads, and said, "God bless you, my boys!" As he passed on, one of the ruffians turned to the other, and said, "He *is* a man, Bill; he *is* a man. *He's a man like God!*"

Was that "serene beauty" on Mr. Wesley's face the playing of an actor's part? Or was it the outer reflection of an inner poise produced by the presence of One who had long ago said: "In the world ye shall have tribulation: but be of good

cheer; I have overcome the world" (John 16: 33)? I think you
know what reply St. Paul would have given. For he enter-
tained no doubt that, even in the presence of monstrous men
and vicious surroundings, there is an answer to the prayer of
the Christian soul:

> *Speak through the earthquake, wind, and fire,*
> *O still small voice of calm.*

Or consider what we may call the *distraction of indiscipline.*
The Phillips translation of verse 11 brings it before us: "Now
we hear that you have some among you living quite undisciplined lives . . . busy only in other people's affairs." This
accounts for the advice given earlier: "don't associate with
the brother whose life is undisciplined" (v. 6).

The "brother" who was "disorderly," to use the word of the
Authorized Version, may have been one of those members of
the Thessalonian congregation who misunderstood the apostolic teaching concerning the Second Advent. Christ's return
is at hand. Our glorification with Him is upon us. Why then
should the ordinary activities and responsibilities of life engage our energies or occupy our minds?

By thus misreading and misapplying the "blessed hope" they
tended to become impractical visionaries who declined duty and
disparaged vocation. What is more, St. Paul implies that when
they were warned against the mistaken course they were pur-
suing, they approved themselves unteachable and opinionated.

It is possible that others were leading "undisciplined" lives
for a more personal and temperamental reason: it was simply
more to their liking.

Now without question the presence of such persons makes
it difficult for those tidy-minded Christians who want some
firmness in their habits and are eager to be commanded by
high loyalties. Haven't all of us felt the sharp edge of the
problem at some time or another? How some folks *do* threaten
to ruffle the pool of our peace!

Mind you, they aren't liars—they are just not careful about
the accuracy of the things they say.

They aren't maliciously rude—they are just negligent about keeping appointments and being on time.

They aren't dishonest—they are just careless and slow in the meeting of their obligations.

They aren't exactly slanderers—they are just thoughtless about other people's reputation and influence.

Disciplined Christians living cheek by jowl with the undisciplined! St. Paul knew the problem. Knowing it, he prayed as he did: "The Lord of peace . . . give you peace."

Or, to name but one more, think of the *distraction of indolence*. Moffatt brings it out vividly in verses 10 and 11: "We used to charge you, even when we were with you, 'If any man will not work, he shall not eat.' But we are informed that some of your number are loafing."

"Drones in the congregational hive," someone has called them! Perhaps we are entitled to whatever comfort there is in the fact that this is not a twentieth-century phenomenon. The industrious Christians of the first century had to live with it and, so far as possible, correct it.

One doesn't have to be a "super-charged engine" of a person, one has only to be normally energetic, to discover how really taxing it is to get on with loafers and dawdlers. It is easy to imagine the scorn with which a producer like Henry Ward Beecher handled the case of a student who wrote him a letter, asking for an "easy berth." Beecher replied:

"Young man, you cannot be an editor; do not try the law; do not think of the ministry; let alone all ships and merchandise; abhor politics; don't practise medicine; be not a farmer, a soldier, or a sailor; don't study; don't think. None of these are easy. Oh, my son, you have come into a hard world. I know of only one easy place in it, and that is in the grave!"

Perhaps the best way to sum up the matter—this reality of Christian peace in the midst of distraction—is to look at the man who is praying for these Thessalonian believers. The rigours of wide travel levied a toll on his body. The heckling of critics rang frequently in his ears. The brutality of his persecutors drew blood from his back. "The care of all the churches" pressed heavily upon his mind. Despite it all, no one spoke more often—nor with greater conviction—about "the peace that passeth understanding." He knew, as we must, that God's peace within us does not require a gilt frame of easy circumstance. Galilee lashed with tempest and Calvary black with sunlessness cannot keep the serene Saviour from saying, "Peace I leave with you, my peace I give unto you" (John 14: 27).

II

Moving now from negatives to positives, we find that it is peace *by means of direction* for which St. Paul is praying: "May the Lord direct your hearts to the love of God and to the steadfastness of Christ" (RSV). Weymouth has "guide your hearts" and Arthur Way "pilot your hearts."

In 1953 Professor Rollo May, of the William Alanson White Institute of Psychiatry in New York, published a book entitled *Man's Search For Himself*. In the opening chapter, on "Loneliness and Anxiety," Dr. May gives it as his opinion that the "chief problem of people in the middle decade of the twentieth century" is the feeling, either vague or acute, of *emptiness* and the sense of *undirectedness*.

He agrees with a fellow-author, David Riesman, who suggests that prior to the first World War the "typical American" was more "inner-directed," whereas since then he has tended to be more "outer-directed." From the psychiatric point of view this "inner-directedness" simply means that one has motives, standards and ambitions which command his respect and significantly shape his outer conduct. "Outer-directness," on the other hand, is the term given to those who, lacking strong subjective convictions, are governed by the pressures, conventions, and desires of those about them. Two mechanical contrivances are used to illustrate these two ways of life: the *gyroscope* and *radar*. The "gyroscope" type of person has an inner stability that makes for calm-mindedness. The "radar" variety, by contrast, is perpetually in stress because he is always getting his directions from others. He has "no effective centre of motivation of his own."

All this, Professor May believes, gives point to the description of modern man, oppressed with the feeling of meaninglessness, that has been given to us by T. S. Eliot:

> *We are the hollow men*
> *We are the stuffed men*
> *Leaning together*
> *Headpiece filled with straw. Alas!*
> *Shape without form, shade without colour,*
> *Paralysed force, gesture without motion; ...*

It is therefore no parson's fancy that moderns on Broadway or Regent Street, no less than ancients on Thessalonica, need someone to pray for them: "And the Lord direct your hearts."

1. Think for a moment of the *sovereignty of the Guide.* "The *Lord* direct!"

Here is where some of us, right at the outset, become "foul balls" in the game of life: we don't want to stay within the guide-lines of fair play. Whoever said, "A man's worst troubles begin when he takes it in hand to do as he pleases," had been reading wisdom out of the book of life. For to be self-ruled means in the end to be self-ruined.

Just as a motor-car was made to run on a fuel which the English call petrol and Americans call gasoline, so human beings were made to run, not on self-will, but on the will of God. Put alcohol or witch hazel in the tank and, no matter how shiny the exterior or elegant the upholstery, the car fails to function.

Which thing is a parable: making one's own will the rule of life stalls life, fouls it up, frustrates it; whereas making God's will the pattern of our living gives meaning, integration, and permanence to what we are and do.

D. H. Lawrence is not always "tailor-made" for quotation by the preacher, but he was on the target when he wrote:

"The modern slave is the man who does not receive his powers from the unseen, and give reverence, but thinks he is his own little boss. Only a slave would take the trouble to shout, 'I am free,' in the face of the open heavens."

Yet worldlings are not the only persons who miss God's calm by missing His control. There are "sons of God" who have their troubles because, though subject to His will in most matters, there are areas and episodes in connection with which an assertive and uncrucified ego bounces out to claim its own. There's an appalling impudence about the self-life. For a long mile it has given no trouble and then, suddenly, at a bend in the road, it clambers up in God's seat and takes the reins. Its subtlety is matched by nothing but its longevity. Even in the life of the Christian it is forever trying to salvage some scrap, some tiny shred, of its own bedraggled dignity. Anything, it is always crying, anything but giving up under the death-blow of the Saviour's Cross!

It is just here, nevertheless, that the God-guided life really comes into its own. George Muller of Bristol testified: "There was a day when I died—died to George Muller, his opinions, preferences, tastes, and will; died to the world, its approval or censure; died to the approval or blame of my brethren and friends; and since then I have studied only to show myself approved unto God."

It was this George Muller who said, in the soft glow of his life's sunset, "I never remember in all my Christian course, a period now of sixty-nine years and four months, that I ever sincerely and patiently sought to know the will of God by the teaching of the Holy Ghost, through the instrumentality of the Word of God, but I have always been directed rightly."

Strong as these words are, they are not a claim to infallibility, errorlessness, or absolute sinlessness. Not at all! Deeply significant, it seems to me, are the qualifying terms that Muller uses: "sincerely and patiently" seeking to "know the will of God." It is this constant bending to Christ's Lordship that makes possible His sovereign control over us, and this gives us our clue to sub-surface serenity of spirit. Charles Wesley would put it this way:

> *Lord, that I may learn of Thee,*
> *Give me true simplicity;*
> *Wean my soul and keep it low,*
> *Willing Thee alone to know.*

> *Let me cast my reeds aside,*
> *All that feeds my knowing pride,*
> *Not to man, but God submit,*
> *Lay my reasonings at Thy feet.*

2. Think, too, of the *sphere of the guidance* for which prayer is made. "The Lord direct your *hearts.*" Owen's comment on the Biblical meaning of "heart" may be helpful here: "The heart in Scripture is variously used, sometimes for the mind and understanding, sometimes for the will, sometimes for the affections, sometimes for the conscience, sometimes for the whole soul. Generally, it denotes the whole soul of man and all the faculties of it."[1]

In agreement with this position are the comments of Dr. Harold Ockenga on the verse before us: "Now when the word 'heart' is used here, it is not only affections, because the word 'heart' in the New Testament involves the will and the mind and the affections."[2]

It is not uncommon for a person to say, "My heart tells me one thing and my head another." Such a sharp distinction is not recognized in the New Testament. A bad heart, in the view of Holy Scripture, is one in which there is bad thinking as well as bad feeling. A good heart, by the same logic, is one in which the mind, no less than the emotions, has been cleansed and surrendered to God. This, at any rate, is the rule. An exception may occur here and there,

---

[1] *International Standard Bible Encyclopedia*, Vol. II, (Eerdmans, Grand Rapids), p. 1351.
[2] Ockenga, *The Church In God*, (Fleming H. Revell, New York), p. 322.

as in the famous passage: "Thou shalt love the Lord thy God with all thy heart, and with all thy soul, and with all thy strength, and with all thy mind" (Luke 10: 27).

Now, since the "Lord" to whom St. Paul refers, must be, in the terms of our experience with Him, the Holy Spirit, it follows that the directed person is one who has made all of his redeemed powers available to the Spirit. What flows from this basic fact is important: there is no one way by which the Holy Spirit guides us, even as there is no one area of our personality—whether mind, emotions, will, imagination, or conscience—within which the direction always comes.

Sometimes the guidance is given through the Bible, sometimes through circumstances, sometimes through the counsel of others, sometimes through reason, sometimes through the Inner Voice.

Where two or more of these "green lights" are lined up together the factor of certitude is made the stronger. Our greatest watchfulness should be exercised in the case of the Inner Voice. Those who practise the art of listening come, in time, to a seasoned recognition of the real thing. They are not easily fooled by the devil's ventriloquy. It is here, nevertheless, that subjective impressions need to be checked against objective authority. If the Voice that is within us speaks contrary to the Bible that is before us, then the Bible's veto on the Voice should be heeded. Even the Bible must be read *from within,* so to speak, in order to get the revelation God has for us in it.. The Scriptures, if taken mechanically or magically, can lead us astray, for they contain the *quoted* words of mistaken or evil men as well as the *inspired* words of "holy men who were moved by the Holy Spirit."

To all of this I think a word should be added that we sometimes overlook: there is the *hidden* direction of our Lord. The yielded heart trusts its Lord for a guidance that is effective even when there is no consciousness of it. Indeed the proof of its effectiveness may not be known until long afterwards. This is what my esteemed friend, J. Danson Smith, has sought to say to us in the simple lines:

> *'Tis good to dwell on years now past,*
> *And on those problem days,*
> *When we could only on Him cast*
> *The future with its maze;*
> *To find He brought us through at last*
> *By unexpected ways.*

3. But the directedness that is linked with serenity takes now another turn in St. Paul's prayer: *the splendour of the goals*. Toward what high objectives does the Lord's direction carry us? It is a double answer that the Apostle gives us: (a) "into the love of God," and (b) "into the patient waiting for Christ."

"*Into* the love of God!" But if we are Christians, aren't we already *there*? Yes, and No! But, surely, if we are unconditionally surrendered Christians in whose hearts the Holy Spirit has indeed "shed abroad" the love of God, we are *there*, are we not? Yes, and No!

If you proceed from Europe to the United States of America, your arrival in New York puts you in the United States. From one point of view you couldn't be any more in it than you are when you are in New York. But if you should make the mistake of thinking that New York *is* the United States, three minutes with a Kansas Cityian or a minute and a half with a San Franciscan will put you right! The United States being so vast a country, you can be in it and yet go *on* in it for a long time and a long distance.

Is it otherwise with the love of God? Here is vastness beyond the penetration of our faltering vision. Here is depth beyond our dreaming. Here is height beyond our scaling.

Do you think of the love of God as *revelation*? If so, you are thinking of the matchless compassion and grace He has

historically unveiled in Jesus Christ, and supremely in the
Cross of Christ. You have seen in that Calvary-grace the
ground and guarantee of your salvation, including that aspect
of salvation that crucially and deeply deals with the insub-
ordination and infection of the self-life. Well and good! But
have you seen all the inwardness of that Cross and the love
it expresses—the cost to God of redeeming wretches like
ourselves, the sheer madness (from our worldly point of view)
of the risks God took and the venture God made in coming
amongst us "made in the likeness of men"?

No, you haven't? Not even a St. John of the Cross or a
St. Teresa or a Fenelon has. When Franz Liszt, the composer,
was near the end of his life, he wrote out a statement directing
the disposition of his personal effects after his death. Then
he added: "I am writing this on the date of September 4, 1860,
when the Church celebrates the elevation of the Holy Cross.
The voice of this feast also expresses the ardent and mysterious emotion which, like sacred stigmata, has trans-pierced
my entire life. Yes, Jesus Christ crucified, the madness and
the elevation of the Cross, this was my true vocation!"[1]

Most of us, reflecting on pulsing sentences such as these,
are made aware of the yet unexplored wonder of God's love
into which He mercifully offers to lead us.

Or, do you think of the love of God as *response*? Here we
interpret the phrase to mean our love for Him rather than
His for us. His love for us in Christ is both sanctuary and
spur. As *sanctuary*, we hide in it and know ourselves to
be safe, let evil rage as it will and temptation beat as it
may.

But as *spur*, the love of God kindles, evokes, challenges. It
calls us to the restful recklessness of giving ourselves away
in His service and kingdom. It calls us to take Him seriously
when He says, "As I have loved you . . . love one another."
It calls us to bend to the yoke when we hear the Saviour
pray, "As thou hast sent me into the world, even so have I
also sent them." It calls us to the calm confidence that when

[1] cf., Stewart, *The Crucifixion In Our Street* (Richard Smith, N.Y.), p. 11.

life is linked and leagued with love, it takes on a permanence,
a magnificent indestructibility, that nothing else can confer
upon it. For,

> *All things that are on earth shall wholly*
> *pass away,*
> *Except the love of God, which shall live*
> *and last for aye.*
>
> .   .   .   .   .
>
> *And the great globe itself, so the Holy*
> *Writings tell,*
> *With the rolling firmament, where the*
> *starry armies dwell,*
> *Shall melt with fervent heat,—they shall*
> *all pass away,*
> *Except the love of God, which shall live*
> *and last for aye."*

Into something as engagingly expansive and enduring as that
the Spirit of the Lord will faithfully direct us.

The other splendid goal of the divine direction is "the
patience of Christ." This rendering is much to be preferred
above that of the King James Version. Other variants are:
"the steadfastness of Christ" (Conybeare), "a steadfastness
like Christ's" (Goodspeed), "a patient endurance like Christ's"
(Williams), and "the patient suffering of Christ" (Phillips).

This quality of "patient endurance," which is part and
parcel of the "mind of Christ" and is communicated to us by
the Holy Spirit of love, needs some careful *interpreting*. It
is not merely the absence of inflammable temper. It is more
than acquiescence in something troublesome or annoying.

Acquiescence can lead to quietism and withdrawal. It can
be a form of escape. Did William Tyndale acquiesce in the
opposition of the King and the "powers that be" to his
proposal to translate the Holy Scriptures into the language
of the English people? Never! He was made of more heroic
stuff. Though his hecklers hounded him and his persecutors
jailed him, he persisted in his purpose. Through it all he

remained, like his Lord, unembittered and undiscouraged. His dying prayer has been called "a classic of English history": "Lord, open the King of England's eyes!"

Acquiescence is too negative and passive. The "patience of Christ" is more positive and redemptive. Acquiescence *submits*; the "patience of Christ" *uses*.

Passive submission in John Bunyan would have had a tinker silently languishing in Bedford jail, whereas the "patience of Christ" in him produced a *Pilgrim's Progress*. When we read in Hebrews 12 : 2 that Jesus "for the joy that was set before him, endured the cross, despising the shame, and is set down on the right hand of the throne of God," the picture we get is perfectly exhilarating. It is not a picture of pious passivity but of creative activity through pain. It is taking thorns and transmuting them into thrones!

Into these clearer insights and deeper experiences God would lead his children; and, leading them, would cause them to know, amid shock and hurt, the under-surface peace that holds.

Not the least of the values in this line of New Testament thinking is precisely this : knowing that trouble and pain are bound to invade the Christian's life, we are forearmed against it and prepared for its rigours. John Newton's lines help us to see it :

> *Why should I complain of want or distress,*
> *Temptation or pain? He told me no less;*
> *The heirs of salvation, I know from His Word,*
> *Through much tribulation must follow their Lord.*

Thus far we have tried to see that the peace for which Paul prays in his affectionate concern for these Thessalonians is a boon they may possess in the midst of distraction and is associated with a sense of divine direction. One more facet of it now lures us.

III

It is peace *in the form of donation* : "Now the Lord of peace himself give you peace always by all means" (v. 16). As

Phillips draws it out, it reads: "Now may the Lord of peace personally give you His peace at all times and in all ways." Then follows the brief benediction: "The Lord be with you all."

Between the peace and the Presence there is an inseparable connection. The Donor is even greater than the donation, the Giver than His gift. To see this, to practise it, to rely on it, is worth more than all the money that all the psychiatrists collect in a year.

Towering and resourceful personalities have a way of lifting their associates out of themselves, calming their fears, inspiring their courage, making them impervious to hardship. Somewhere I have read of a letter that one of Lord Nelson's men wrote after a particularly tough assignment had been carried through by the British navy. A Spanish fleet nearly twice the size of Nelson's had been put "on the run" and pursued to the West Indies. One of his commanders, Robert Stopford, wrote: "We are half starved, and otherwise inconvenienced by being so long out of port. But our reward is—we are with Nelson!"

Is that understandable? If so, then let no one doubt that a greater than Nelson—the "Lord of peace," the "Prince of peace"—can, by His unfailing presence, subdue our fears, chase away our boredoms, discipline our suspicions, quiet our anxieties, and garrison our hearts with His own serenity.

He is *incessantly* the Donor of peace: "at all times."

He is *ingeniously* the Donor of peace: "in all ways."

As to the latter, Maclaren gives it as his view that St. Paul's reference is "not so much to the various manners in which the divine peace is bestowed, as to the various aspects that peace is capable of assuming."

If the point is allowed—and I think it makes no great difference—the beneficently ingenious workings of the unpanicked Christ are still to be recognized.

Did *He* not find the Father's nearness so perpetually renewed to Him in the days of His flesh that no shadow could

terrify Him and no foe daunt Him? Noisy and demanding
crowds might weary Him, but a tryst with the Father renewed
Him. Ailing creatures of all sorts—leprous, sightless, and
lonely—might steal "virtue" from Him, but repairing to the
place of prayer brought its healing calm to His nerves and
feelings. Cunning shysters in religion, crafty veterans in
politics, and just plain mad-men of the mob might make the
night hideous with their scorn of justice and their scream of
hate, but the confidence of the Father's unforsaking presence
centrally held Him.

And now, with all that behind Him (though forever a part
of Him), He says to you and to me, in all the varied strains
and stresses of our days, "Peace I leave with you, my peace I
give unto you: not as the world giveth, give I unto you. Let
not your heart be troubled, neither let it be afraid."

What answer will you give to *that*? Make it personal. St.
Paul did. He wanted these Thessalonians to do it.

What better answer can you give than to say: "It is enough,
Lord. It is enough! Thy presence and Thy peace!"

> *And all the jarring notes of life*
> *Seem blending in a psalm,*
> *And all the angles of its strife*
> *Slow rounding into calm.*
>
> *And so the shadows fall apart,*
> *And so the west winds play;*
> *And all the windows of my heart*
> *I open to the day."*